W9-DED-234

THE BEST INTERESTS OF CHILDREN:
AN EVIDENCE-BASED APPROACH

A common lament among commentators on child custody law is the dearth of information about children's best interests. Even rarer are guidelines that are backed by population-based empirical evidence. This book attempts to explain child custody outcomes in Canada in terms of factors that predict legal behaviour and factors that are empirically associated with beneficial outcomes for children. In particular the study examines the relative weight that should be placed on such matters as family structure, household income, parental education, and parental gender on the best interests of children. These predictors are tested with the National Longitudinal Survey of Children and Youth, a statistical model using a very large sample of Canadian children, aged 4 to 11 years. The study also uses data from Canada's Centre for Justice Statistics to understand the predictors of custody outcomes in Canada for a five-year period. A key finding is that parental gender plays an important role in determining custody outcomes in Canada, but is not important for children's outcomes. A separate study of child support and household income is also included.

The Best Interests of Children provides a wealth of evidence and suggests a new paradigm and series of criteria for assessing child custody. It fills a gap in the Canadian family law landscape and will be invaluable not only to the academic community in the areas of law, social work, psychology, sociology, and family studies, but also to the wide array of legal and mental health professionals involved in assisting children and families in the divorce process where child custody is at issue.

PAUL MILLAR is a postdoctoral fellow in the Department of Community Health Sciences at Brock University.

PAUL MILLAR

The Best Interests of Children

An Evidence-Based Approach

UNIVERSITY OF TORONTO PRESS
Toronto   Buffalo   London

© University of Toronto Press Incorporated 2009
Toronto Buffalo London
www.utppublishing.com
Printed in Canada

ISBN 978-0-8020-9890-0 (cloth)
ISBN 978-0-8020-9593-0 (paper)

Printed on acid-free paper

Library and Archives Canada Cataloguing in Publication

Millar, Paul, 1955–
The best interests of children : an evidence-based approach / Paul Millar.

Includes bibliographical references and index.
ISBN 978-0-8020-9890-0 (bound). ISBN 978-0-8020-9593-0 (pbk.)

1. Custody of children – Canada. 2. Divorce – Law and legislation –
Canada. 3. Child support – Law and legislation – Canada. 4. Children of
divorced parents – Canada. I. Title.

KE600.M54 2009   346.7101'73   C2009-904727-6
KF547.M54 2009

This book has been published with the help of a grant from the Canadian
Federation for the Humanities and Social Sciences, through the Aid to
Scholarly Publications Programme, using funds provided by the Social
Sciences and Humanities Research Council of Canada.

University of Toronto Press acknowledges the financial assistance to its
publishing program of the Canada Council for the Arts and the Ontario
Arts Council.

University of Toronto Press acknowledges the financial support for its
publishing activities of the Government of Canada through the
Book Publishing Industry Development Program (BPIDP).

To Vanessa, Jason, Lisa, Camille, and Valerie

There is no independent measure of each child's best interests against which to measure the actual outcomes in disputed cases.
—Eleanor E. Maccoby and Robert H. Mnookin, *Dividing the Child*

... there is a paucity of relevant research evidence on which to base the practice of child custody evaluations ...
—James G. Byrne et al., 'Practitioner Review'

Contents

Tables and Figures

Figures

Appendix

Acknowledgments

I am indebted to many people who helped me on my way to publishing this book. First and foremost, I want to thank Dr Augustine Brannigan, who gave me many suggestions that improved the quality of the work and whose prodding set me on the path to publication. He was generous with his guidance, keen insight, and support.

This book is derived from a PhD dissertation written at the University of Calgary, Canada. Many people read earlier draughts and made comments and suggestions that improved the quality of this work. These include Dr Erin Gibbs Van Brunschot, Dr Richard Wanner, and Dr Louis Knafla of the University of Calgary, and Dr Murray Straus of the University of New Hampshire. Anonymous reviewers were also of great assistance in giving the book more focus and making it more accessible.

I was also fortunate to benefit generally from the community of scholars at the University of Calgary, who provided me with the tools and training I needed to develop the material presented here. Many faculty members gave generously of their support and guidance, including Dr Tom Langford, Dr Anne Gauthier, Dr Leslie Miller, Dr Sheldon Goldenberg, Dr Lloyd Wong, Dr Daniel Béland, Dr Ariel Ducey, Dr Cora Voyageur, and Dr Jim Frideres. I am also indebted to Dr Terrance Wade of Brock University.

I am also grateful to the freedom of information office of Canada's Department of Justice, who facilitated the release of a large file of divorce information that enabled an important part of the analysis in this book. The people who help the public access government information perform an invaluable service to the public, and, ultimately, to the government itself. Live long and prosper.

Finally, I am most grateful to my family, who put up with me as I worked on this book. My wife, Valerie, read many early drafts, helped improve the text, and, most importantly, tolerated the irregularities of a graduate student's life. Thank you.

THE BEST INTERESTS OF CHILDREN:
AN EVIDENCE-BASED APPROACH

1 Introduction

I have been researching the area of family law in Canada for several years, with a particular emphasis on custody determinations (Millar and Goldenberg 1998, 2004) and some incursion into the area of child support (Millar and Gauthier 2002). That research highlighted a couple of surprising facts: first, the Canadian legal system holds the 'best interests of the child' as the paramount criterion in assessing family law issues, trumping or avoiding even constitutional provisions,[1] and, second, legal commentators lament the dearth of solid criteria available to define what that 'best interests' entails (McLeod and Mamo 2001). Moreover, in an age of constitutional guarantees of gender equality, there is an unusually large imbalance in the awards of custody to mothers compared to fathers. This previous work led to the central questions being explored here: What is in the best interests of children? Can the apparent reliance on gender noted in previous research be explained by differences in parenting or other characteristics that are correlated with gender? Are there other factors that explain the custody outcomes found in previous work that render the effect of gender less important or even spurious? By pursuing these main questions, I hope to better understand what specifically is in children's interests, whether the courts are in fact using criteria that correlate with children's best interests, and, if not, the actions which can be taken to improve the courts' effect on children over time. The importance of tackling this issue has been growing, partly because the number of children affected by divorce is large, but also because the courts and related institutions such as support enforcement agencies are experiencing a growing involvement in the regulation of family life after divorce. The transformation of children from economic to emotional assets (Zelizer 1985) has provided much of the context required to enable state intervention on their behalf. As state intervention proceeds, so does the requirement that it do so in a way that causes the least amount of harm that is consistent with its objectives. Although divorce has long been associated with deficits for children, it may be that the state interventions associated with divorce are part of the reason these deficits are apparent.

Although the large numbers of divorces involving children have only been seen since Canada's first Divorce Act (1968), which established several new criteria for divorce, the courts have, for centuries, made custody determinations (Goldstein and Fenster 1994). These decisions have been guided by presumptions that have varied over time, originating with a paternal presumption that was gradually changed over time to a maternal presumption in the eighteenth and nineteenth centuries, through legislation such as the British Talford's Act (1839), which allowed mothers to petition for the custody of their young children, and the judicially developed maternal case law presumption called the 'Tender Years Doctrine,' which presumed that young children should be placed with their mothers (Millar and Goldenberg 2004). This latter maternal presumption appears to have been in place in Canada since at least the beginning of the twentieth century (Snell 1991:196), and remained in place until the formal introduction of the 'best interests' standard through Canada's second Divorce Act (1986). This second federal statute was enacted in the aftermath of the introduction of the Canadian Charter of Rights and Freedoms (1982), and its wording reflects a careful consideration for gender neutrality, which might be expected considering the emphasis on gender equality in the Charter.[2] Paradoxically, the introduction of this legislation with its gender-neutrality coincided with a proportionally larger share of sole custody to the mother, best explained by the introduction of social context education of the judiciary that emphasized the unfairness to mothers of legal custody outcomes (Millar and Goldenberg 1998). The foregoing suggests a legal system in Canada which has, fairly recently, embarked on a major expansion of family law that has historically placed considerable reliance on parental gender for custody decisions. The introduction of modern ideas of gender neutrality has made little discernible impact on this apparent reliance despite a manifest policy of the gender-neutral standard that is the 'best interests of the child.' However, the assertion that the correlation of parental gender with custody outcomes is necessarily against children's interests is supported only by very simple, mostly bivariate, analyses, so the question of whether other variables account for some or most of the relationship between custody outcome and parental gender remains unanswered. Moreover, the data needed to do a more sophisticated analysis was possessed only by the Central Divorce Registry of the Canadian Department of Justice.

As the result of a freedom of information request, I was able to obtain this data from the Department of Justice in raw form. The analysis of the data, presented in Chapter 2, is the first such analysis of custody data published to date, and the first attempt at predicting legal case outcomes using multivariate modelling techniques. Since multivariate modelling allows the estimation of the effects of a particular variable, such as gender, controlling for the effects of other variables, it enables stronger claims about the causal relationship between parental gender and the custody case outcome. However, a greater problem remains in demonstrating the connection or lack thereof of parental gender to the best interests of children: the best interests of children and their predictors have not been established. This is not to say that various communities do not have ideas about what issues are important in creating benefits for children: the frameworks employed by the legal, psychological, and sociological communities largely ignore each other and use different theoretical paradigms and different approaches to empirical investigations. The empirical investigations of the legal and psychological communities are based on the analysis of particular cases that have come into the court or clinic, while most sociological investigations are constructed in a manner designed to produce estimates of the population.

Chapter 3 investigates the theoretical perspectives used by such agents as custody evaluators and legal actors, as well as the empirical evidence available related to divorce and its effects on children, in order to understand the perspectives adopted by the communities involved with custody decision-making and to develop theoretical expectations for the empirical inquiries in subsequent chapters. In order to measure the best interests of children, this book takes the position that factors determining children's interests and consequent custody should be those that demonstrably affect children's behaviour, health, and educational success. This emphasis on measuring the child is meant to ensure that the dependent variable(s) in the analysis are valid: they measure what is intended. Other factors, even if previously found to be correlated with children's best interests are not used as surrogates and must compete for explanatory power among the other factors measured in the analysis.

The best available data in Canada for understanding the success of children is the National Longitudinal Survey of Children and Youth (NLSCY) conducted by Statistics Canada, which follows a large number of children over time and measures a wide range of attributes of these children's lives. The data from this survey is maintained by Statistics Canada, and, in order to ensure that its guarantees of confidentiality to respondents are kept, does not allow non-employees to work with any of the raw data from the survey.[3] To achieve access to this data, I applied and was granted the status of a 'deemed' employee of Statistics Canada, which entailed submitting a proposal to be approved through a peer-review process, swearing an oath to maintain the confidentiality of the data, and being subject to criminal penalties should I fail to do so. Further, all work with this data was conducted on secure physical premises controlled by Statistics Canada in their Prairie Regional Data Centre at the University of Calgary. All results based on Statistics Canada data discussed in this work have been reviewed by Statistics Canada personnel before release to ensure that respondent confidentiality is not compromised. A relevant component of this data, an addendum to the NLSCY called the custody file, provides measures related to child access or visitation after divorce. Since this was a key concept with respect to the welfare of children under the influence of family law, I had hoped to use this data in conjunction with the other measures in the NLSCY in order to see how access might affect children. Unfortunately, this portion of the survey had been improperly conducted and much of the data was missing, because a significant proportion of the respondents were not asked some of the questions due to errors programmed into the flow of the questions. However, I was able to show that a large enough sample could be created if the missing values were filled in for values that did not change over time. That is, if a value was missing from the second contact with a household, the value from the first contact could be used if the question was related to something that had occurred before the first contact, such as children's birthdays or the time of a marital break-up if the break-up occurred prior to the first contact or cycle. Unfortunately, the officials from Statistics Canada were uncomfortable with this procedure and refused to allow the use of this data. The investigation of the effect of access on the best interests of children is left for future research.

The multivariate models estimating the factors that affect children's outcomes are studied in Chapter 4. This series of models looks not only at the factors that influence children's behaviour, health, and educational performance, but also the causal mechanism involved. In other words, Chapter 4 inquires into *how* these factors create their effects. While this analysis allows the assessment of predictors of children's outcomes – the 'best interests' criterion – there is no measure of the effects of child support in the models presented in Chapter 4, a limitation of the NLSCY dataset which only allowed testing of the effects of household income.

In order to explore the contribution of financial child support to household income, another Statistics Canada dataset had to be employed: the Survey of Labour and Income Dynamics (SLID). Chapter 5 uses this data to gain a basic understanding of the importance of child support to the household income of both paying and receiving households. While the analysis presented here is basic, it is the first attempt to gauge the effects of child support on household income in Canada using a dataset representative of the population.

Chapter 6 has the task of pulling together the results of the separate studies that make up the bricolage that is this book. The conclusions drawn in this chapter are meant to inform potential reforms to family law and to add to the understanding of how the family contributes to child development.

I sincerely hope this book accomplishes these tasks, and provides some light as society struggles to understand what is in the best interests of children.

2 Child Custody Outcomes in Canada

In this chapter, I look at the law within the greater context of social control, and then examine custody within its historical context as a special case of formal social control. The determinants of custody are then tested with a quantitative model using data obtained from the Canadian Department of Justice.

Very few people directly encounter formal law in any given week in a modern industrial state, yet a high degree of social control over a wide variety of behaviours is maintained through legal control, mostly invisibly. Even the United States, one of the most (formally) litigious countries in the world, has only one judge for roughly every 17,000 people while the number of judges in Japan is three times smaller on a per capita basis (Kato 1987). Regardless of this ratio, it represents a large degree of influence for a small number of people, which consequently elevates the importance of judicial behaviour in society. How does such a minuscule group of people maintain so much control?

The judicial arm of the government is a hierarchical power relation with the judgments of lower courts subject to review by higher courts, decisions being 'structured by the entire judicial hierarchy' (Haire, Linquist, and Songer 2003:164). Lawyers, at least indirectly, are subject to the judgment of the court, and, although not directly responsible to courts in the sense that an employee is to a supervisor, nevertheless must understand and predict the likely behaviour of judges and practice within the limits defined by the expected judicial behaviour. This would appear to apply not only to divorce, but to other kinds of cases as well. For instance, Brannigan and Levy (1983) examine plea bargaining in Canada and find that the negotiations are framed by the legal and substantive issues expected to be encountered in court, rather than simply by expediency. In other words, the expected or predicted result in a court of law is of utmost impact, given the reality that most cases do not reach a courtroom. This prediction has been defined as the de facto law: '... a legal duty so-called is nothing but a prediction that if a man does or omits certain things he will be made to suffer in this or that way by way of judgment of the court; – and so of a legal right' (Holmes 1897:458).

The shaping of predictions is a mechanism by which the influence of the court is propagated through professionals such as lawyers. To illustrate: Sarat and Felstiner (1995) describe the traditional lawyer-client relationship where the lawyer 'governs the relationship, defines the terms of interaction, and is responsible for the service provided ... case development and strategy [is] unidirectional ... Lawyers exercise power by manipulating their clients' definitions of the situation and of their role'(20). For example, a non-custodial father might illustrate how he is a 'good father' by the way he makes his child's meals or takes her to school in the morning. His lawyer must explain that the main legal criterion for the establishment of the 'good father' category is the amount and timeliness of the support he pays; no amount of direct care will overcome deficiencies in the area of payments. In other words, the definition of reality flows outward from the courts, with very little opportunity for resistance by the individuals involved. Legal definitions, not individual or common sense definitions, prevail. In this way, lawyers truly function as officers of the court.

This role of propagating the influence of the law extends beyond those who have hired lawyers to completely negotiate or litigate their divorces. There is a continuum of legal involvement which can entail less intensive involvement of lawyers, other quasi-legal actors such as mediators or paralegals, as well as social networks that transmit the influence of the law. Even in situations where the involvement of formal legal actors is minimal or absent, the law sets the context for the parameters of the result. Mnookin and Kornhauser (1979) describe this as 'bargaining in the shadow of the law' in the case of divorce negotiations. That is, although most divorce cases are not decided pursuant to a trial, the negotiations are yet governed by the expected results in a court of law since either party has recourse to that alternative if it is in their interest to do so. I belabour this point a little because very few cases of divorce in Canada are contested to the point of a trial. A study of divorces by the Department of Justice found that on average only 4 per cent of cases involved a 'contested hearing' or trial (Department of

Justice, Canada 1990). This average hides a good deal of variation among provinces. For example, in Alberta and Manitoba only 1 per cent of divorces involved a trial, while in Newfoundland the figure was 11 per cent; the figure for New Brunswick was 21 per cent. Given the small proportion of cases involving a formal trial at court, it is important to understand the highly influential nature of the cases decided there. Cases involving varying degrees of involvement from legal actors, be they judges, lawyers, mediators, paralegals, or even lay persons giving informal advice, are strongly affected by the likely outcome in a court of law.[1] Regardless of the degree of formal legal involvement, law and the courts are highly influential in the process. The dominance of courts over the entire legal process is further accentuated by a structural situation that tends to reflect the interests of the lawyers and courts instead of the interests of the parties involved in divorce.

For most people, divorce is an infrequent occurrence that can have a significant impact on their lives. The interests of the two people divorcing is in obtaining the most advantageous settlement that the given circumstances and legal framework will allow. The interest of their lawyers, however, is largely unaligned with their clients. Unlike lawyers in some fields such as corporate law, where they are dependent on the approval of their clients for future business success, most divorce lawyers handle a large number of clients in a given year. The success of a divorce lawyer depends not so much on any single individual client, but more so on how the lawyer is perceived by judges and by colleagues, that is, other divorce lawyers. In other words, the allegiance of most divorce lawyers lies more with the legal system than with a particular client. Gallanter (1974) describes clients of divorce lawyers as 'one-shotters.' The 'one-shotter' has little interest in attempting to play for a rule change that will help similarly situated people in the long run, since the main interest is his or her immediate case. Over time, this leads the law to be formed in the interests of those for whom the long-term direction of legal rules in divorce is more salient: courts and the lawyers who serve them. People attempting to negotiate a divorce are therefore even more subject to the boundaries of the law than those in some other legal circumstances: they have little interest in changing the rules of the game and so are forced to accept the definition of the situation as it is defined by the courts and their legal representation. Given this structural disadvantage, the influence of the courts is stronger than in other situations where individuals are attempting to negotiate a settlement.

Divorce is costly for the people undergoing it. Where once there was a single house and shared costs of living, most costs – both in time and money – of supporting the same family are now doubled. Moreover, the cost of legal involvement is a strain for all but the wealthiest individuals. Divorcing couples, especially those with children, are consequently not in a position to offer resistance to the legal context in which they find themselves. More importantly, the context ensures that the rules, both formal and informal, will ultimately reflect the interests of judges and lawyers as opposed to the subjects of the divorce process. Change in divorce law that reflects the interests of the participants must come from an external source. The structural and institutional momentum of family law has, in this way, perhaps been an accelerating factor to the diminishing role of the institution of family in favour of legal institutions. Legal institutions are one among many forces that enable social control in modern society.

Social control is accomplished through a combination of formal and informal mechanisms that work in concert. Non-governmental, or informal, social control is achieved through institutions such as religious and ethnic communities, social class, and, of particular interest here, the family. As law enters areas that these institutions influence, the law will expand to take their place and consequently these institutions will weaken. For example, labour unions have weakened in terms of their influence as labour legislation has been enacted that provides many of the protections that once were only available through organized labour. These institutions can be weakened to the point of what Beck and Beck-Gernsheim (2002) call 'zombie categories,' since they still exist but no longer have the life they once did.

Probably the greatest expansion of law in North America in the latter portion of the twentieth century has been in the area of family life, creating a whole new category of judges, lawyers, and associated professionals. Law has entered the family in penal law – in the prosecution of domestic violence – as well as in non-penal law in areas such as child custody, access, and child support, among other areas; thus, the family is consequently much less a factor in informal social control than previously. Since the influence of law has increased, it, therefore, is more important to the welfare of children and is one of the reasons why understanding what the best interests of children is may have important implications for the law as it applies to families. In this case, the law enters the picture by assigning the degree to which each divorcing parent performs the parenting role, and by arranging and enforcing financial transfers between the two households. Judicial decisions, which are magnified in their influence through their effect on decisions negotiated in the shadow of the law, may particularly benefit from knowledge of factors that are empirically related to beneficial outcomes for children.

History of Custody Law

Canadian law uses the 'common law' legal tradition, which derives law from both the written law – statutes – and from common law, also known as case law, precedent, or judge-made law (Boyd 1995). The latter term is sometimes used for precedent because judgments for situations that can be distinguished from those covered by legislation and previous decisions allow judges to create new rules for situations as they arise. Custody law derives from both legislation and precedent; however, as we shall see, precedent is the stronger of these two. Precedent in turn can often be affected by custom, that is, the routine practice of local common people. While this is less the case for procedural law, custom often had a profound effect on substantive legal matters, such as the protection of the property rights of wives (Knafla 1990).

One of the first examples of judge-developed case law, varying from official or legislated legal norms with respect to custody, arose in the 1700s in Britain.[2] At that time 'the father was considered the parent naturally endowed to have custody of the children' (MacDonald 1986:10), and as such a father's right to his children was, in theory, absolute. Yet, in practice, courts 'regularly granted mothers' requests to restrain fathers from interfering with the custody of their children' (Abramowicz 1999). Two examples of these early precedents, in 1763 and 1774, illustrate how judicial discretion allowed fathers to be denied custody, using grounds of what, in modern terms, might be described as child abuse (Goldstein and Fenster 1994). These precedents developed in the aftermath of the Industrial Revolution, which separated the roles of men and women, often severely decreasing the amount of daily contact men had with their children. In this context, legal commentary of the time suggested that 'it was considered ungentlemanly, and even immoral, to deprive mothers of access to their children without good cause' (Bailey 1995). Thus, the behaviour fostered by legal culture, informed more by custom than by the written legal standards of that time, appears to have supported more equal outcomes for mothers than formal legal doctrine might suggest.

This legal environment appears to have presaged the first custody law in Britain, which for the first time provided legislative grounds for awarding custody to mothers. An Act to Amend the Law Relating to the Custody of Infants (1839) (Talfourd's Act) allowed a mother to petition for custody of her young children if she had not committed adultery.[3] A similar act followed in (Upper) Canada in 1855 (Custody of Infants Act). While there are no statistical studies of custody outcomes in Canada prior to 1900,[4] the first decades of the twentieth century exhibit the development of a strong maternal custody preference, with the mother or her family receiving custody in roughly three-quarters of the cases (Snell 1991:196). There appears to have been no change in this preference (except, perhaps, to strengthen it) until the enactment of Canada's second Divorce Act, proclaimed in 1986. Therefore, Canada has had a pronounced maternal custody preference in living memory, even though there were no statutes that specified preference for one parent or the other.

In this way, the legal environment relating to custody has largely been shaped and controlled through judge-made law – legal concepts and presumptions developed through precedent – rather than by legislation.

I turn now from the historical legal environment relating to custody, to the variables potentially correlated with custody outcomes, and the ways of defining custody itself.

Varieties of Custody

There are two main types of custody: residential (or physical) custody and legal custody. Residential custody refers to the place where the child lives on a day-to-day basis. If substantially with one parent only (usually defined as more than 60 per cent of the time, since the child support guidelines use this as a demarcation), the arrangement is considered to be *sole physical custody* or *sole residency*. If the physical location of the child is mostly shared (where the child resides with neither parent more than 60 per cent of the time), the arrangement is referred to as *joint physical custody* or *joint residency*. Legal custody, on the other hand, entails certain rights of the parent with respect to decisions regarding the medical, educational, and religious upbringing of the child. It is in the latter sense that custody will be treated here. The rights of parents with legal custody of their children legally entitle them to access to information about their children from health and educational institutions. The most common situation where there is joint legal custody is where the mother has sole residential custody of the children (Department of Justice, Canada 1990:116). So while joint legal custody is in theory a gender neutral outcome, it may mask an outcome that is far from gender neutral in terms of the involvement of both parents in the lives of their children.

Gaining and Losing Custody

Legal custody of a child is established at birth in a manner that is contingent upon the parent's gender. The mother of a newborn child in Canada obtains custody of a child upon his or her birth. A man may obtain custody of a newborn child in three main ways: through a relationship with the child's mother at or near the time of the child's birth (defined in various ways, such as marriage, cohabitation, or a relationship of some permanence); by claiming parentage on the child's birth certificate (with the mother's permission); or by an order of the court (Family Law Act 2003; Holland 2000:136). Hence, the legal framework assures the child has one legal parent (the mother), with a potential for one other contingent on the social circumstances surrounding the birth.[5] The custodial parent or parents then retain custody unless it is severed in one of four ways: in the child's interests (usually through the involvement of a child protection agency); upon the child's living independently; at the age of majority of the child, if competent; or at the point of divorce, through an order for sole custody to the other parent. Thus, a custody determination pursuant to divorce is not so much a decision to award custody, but a decision regarding from whom to remove it. Because of the way that law is propagated through legal and quasi-legal actors, law influences the outcome of custody determinations even though the vast majority of divorce cases are settled out of court and only ratified or approved by a judge after agreement has been reached.

I now turn to a discussion of how the involvement of the law fluctuates for an individual divorce or custody negotiation.

Involvement of the Law in the Determination of Custody

The determination of legal custody of a child after divorce can entail a varying amount of legal involvement. The minimum amount of legality occurs when the parents agree on the terms of the custody of the child between themselves, without the involvement of lawyers and without any formal registration of this agreement with the court. In this situation, which only happens when a formal divorce is not required or where the parents were never married, both parents retain full legal custody of their child since a court order is required to change legal custodial status. In this case, legal norms impinge on the custody negotiations indirectly only in so much as each partner is aware of them. This situation is only tenable where the custodial parent does not apply for social assistance, since these agencies require disclosure of any party liable for support payments. It also means that any exchange of child support cannot be enforced by a provincial enforcement agency. Hence, few relationship dissolutions avoid the impingement of some aspect of the formal legal process; the 'shadow of the law' (Mnookin and Kornhauser 1979) falls on nearly all. Divorce negotiations are framed and shaped by the perception of the parties concerning what results might be achieved if either one resorted to greater legal involvement.

Slightly more legal involvement occurs if the agreement is registered with the court, again without the involvement of any third party. This necessarily involves some direct legal impact on the outcome, since a judge must sign the agreement. Although the judge may never see either of the parties, the agreement must be within acceptable legal parameters before the order will be signed, and, hence, come into force. For example, if there is an amount for child support specified, it must agree with the amount set out in the child support guidelines or risk not being approved, since these amounts are presumptive (Divorce Act 1986: ss.11(1)(b) & 15(1)(3)). Moreover, the divorce must be filed in the form required by the court and be accompanied by the fee required to open a case, thus requiring at least minimal knowledge or guidance from a legal practitioner. In this way, the 'shadow of the law' has gradations that depend on the degree of both formal and informal networks and other resources that influence the parties, even if no legal counsel is directly involved (Jacob 1992).

Legal involvement can increase from the consultation of lawyers by one or both parties, to interim hearings regarding issues in the divorce, to a full trial. Any custody order that is not arrived at as a result of a trial before a judge is referred to as a *consent order*. The vast preponderance of all orders for child custody are consent orders. Although described as 'consent' orders, this does not imply that these orders were entered into freely; either party could avail themselves of a court hearing if agreement was not reached, and this eventuality figures into the negotiations that lead to such agreements.

Unit of Analysis and Custody Outcomes

The unit of analysis for custody studies, such as the one being contemplated here, is the parent-child relationship, since custody determinations necessarily entail a choice, usually between one of two parent-child relationships. Possible outcomes of the custody determination for a given child may be *sole custody*, where one parent retains all legal rights and responsibilities towards the child while most rights and some responsibilities are severed for the other parent; or *joint custody*, where both parents retain all legal rights and responsibilities. Joint custody has become more prevalent since the mid-1980s. Although it was theoretically possible for a judge to order it before then, this was rarely done before the implementation of Canada's second Divorce Act (1986), which specifically identifies joint custody as a possible outcome (s.16(4)). The rights and responsibilities of a 'non-custodial' parent may vary, depending on the specific arrangements for the child. For example, if a non-custodial parent has court-ordered access (or visitation), whereby he or she can temporarily parent the child, then the 1986 Divorce Act provides for that parent to be allowed access to medical and educational information about his or her child (s.16(5).[6] However, for the purposes of this study, if one parent is awarded sole custody the other is considered to have no custody. Thus, when the unit of analysis is the parent-child relationship (as opposed to the child), there are three possible outcomes: sole custody, joint custody, or no custody.

Another variety of custody – split custody – is possible when the unit of analysis is the family. Split custody refers to the custodial assignment where some of the children in a family are placed in the custody of one parent and some in the custody of the other. Split custody appears to be rarely ordered: Ackerman and Ackerman (1997) report that American psychologists recommend it in 6 per cent of cases, and Ackerman (2001) cites two unpublished studies that indicated family law judges and attorneys expect this outcome in only 4.4 per cent and 3.8 per cent of cases, respectively. Similarly, a study by the Canadian Department of Justice found that 22 of 559, or 3.9 per cent, of custody cases sampled from the late 1980s resulted in split custody (Department of Justice, Canada 1990:103). In any event, since split custody requires the unit of analysis to be the family, it is not a possible outcome where the unit of analysis is the parent-child relationship, and so will not be an outcome in the analysis under consideration.

Gender

Previous studies have noted a pronounced gender imbalance in custody decisions in both Canada and the United States (Fox and Kelly 1995; Maccoby and Mnookin 1992; Millar and Goldenberg 1998; Prentice 1979). Although the judicially developed principle of the 'Tender Years Doctrine,' whereby mothers were considered more suitable parents for young children, was considered the norm in common law traditions until recently, divorce law in Canada became gender-neutral from the point of view of legislation with the introduction of the second Divorce Act (1986), which contains no mention of 'husband,' 'wife,' 'mother,' 'father,' or any other gendered term.

The 'tender years' maternal presumption was a judicially developed concept which arose in British law beginning in the eighteenth century (Abramowicz 1999). This preference appears to have been well established in Canada since the beginning of the twentieth century, at least empirically: about three-quarters of cases between 1900 and 1939 favoured mothers or their families over fathers or their families (Snell 1991). Moreover, there appears to be no evidence of a change in this gender preference since that time, and the comparatively recent change in legislation does not appear to have had an immediate impact on the gender imbalance in custody decisions. For example, Millar and Goldenberg (1998) actually note an increase in the gender imbalance with respect to custody outcomes at the time of the introduction of Canada's second Divorce Act, which they attribute to a judicial education program that taught judges that custody decisions were being unfairly biased against mothers. (For an example of this empirically challenged material see McBean 1987.) Despite this apparently continuing near-universal maternal preference in custody outcomes, psychologists performing custody evaluations regard the gender of the parent among the least relevant considerations in custody decisions (Ackerman and Ackerman 1997; Warshak 1993).

This study will consider other factors (aside from gender) to see which predictors account for custody determination outcomes.

Who Files for Divorce and Why?

Previous studies have documented an effect of taking the legal role of the petitioner or plaintiff (the initial person filing for divorce), as opposed to the respondent on custody, with petitioners having a distinct advantage in obtaining custody of their children (Friedman and Percival 1976; Prentice 1979). Moreover, there is a consistent gender imbalance in divorce filings, with women far more likely to petition for divorce than are men. For example, in the years 1970 to 1985, women were the petitioners in 60 to 64 per cent of divorces (Department of Justice, Canada 1990:37). This is true not only in Canada, but in the United States as well: from 1975 to 1988, wives were 64.9 to 71.4 per cent of petitioners in divorces with children present compared with 25.6 to 28.8 per cent of husbands (the balance were jointly initiated). Wives were less likely to be petitioners when children were absent: 56.1 to 62.0 per cent during the same period (National Center for Health Statistics 1996:218). Indeed, historically, 60 per cent of divorces in the United States were initiated by wives in the period 1778 to 1866, and at even higher rates during the period 1867 to 1931 (Friedman and Percival 1976).

Although simply initiating the divorce does not necessarily mean that that party is the one initiating the dissolution of the marriage, an American study of divorce found that, based on reports of both husbands and wives, wives were about twice as likely as husbands to initiate the marital dissolution (Braver and O'Connell 1998). This finding lends credence to the assertion that wives are not only more likely to initiate the legal proceedings, but are also more likely to initiate the dissolution of the marriage. Brinig and Allen (2000) attribute this gender imbalance in filing for divorce to the imbalance in custody likelihood; that is, women are more likely to file for divorce because they are more likely to retain the most important asset of the marriage: the children. Whatever the cause, however, the disparity in propensity to file for divorce is indisputable: women file for divorce at rates far exceeding those for men and seem to have done so as far back as historical records have been kept.

Characteristics of the Children

There have been only a few findings with respect to the characteristics of children and their effects on the custody determination process. For example, Maccoby and Mnookin (1992) found that the age and sex of children had an effect on the physical custody arrangements after divorce. In their study, girls were slightly more likely to live with their mothers than were boys, while the reverse was true of boys with respect to their fathers. Consistent with the ideas underlying the 'Tender Years Doctrine,' infants and toddlers 'almost always lived with their mothers'(779). Further, as children aged in this study, they were less likely to reside jointly with both parents. Regarding the age at which children should be able to make their own decision about their living arrangements, psychologists performing custody evaluations felt, on average, that children should be placed with the parent of their choice once they had reached the age of 15 (Ackerman and Ackerman 1997). The age of the oldest child was positively correlated with an increase in the likelihood of paternal custody in a sample of 509 divorces in the United States, again potentially reflective of the vestiges of the 'tender years' presumption (Fox and Kelly 1995).

The next section outlines the data used to investigate Canadian custody decisions and how it will be analysed.

Data and Method

The dataset for this study was obtained from the Canadian Department of Justice pursuant to a request by this author under Canada's Freedom of Information Act in order to identify the determinants of child custody in Canada. The Department consolidates information on each divorce case in Canada based on data received from each province. The data obtained includes all records kept by the Department of Justice, from Confederation to the end of September 2002, with the exception of fields that might identify an individual case.[7] Thus, the dataset has information on every divorce in Canada, but without the names or the exact birth dates of the parties being divorced: 2,554,271 divorces in all. Only divorces involving children and adjudicated under Canada's second Divorce Act, proclaimed on 1 June 1986, were considered. The parent-child relation was the unit of analysis; thus, there were two records for each child of divorce included in the data (one for the mother-child and one for the father-child relationship). After processing, as outlined in Appendix 1, the data resulted in 1,346,900 records representing 673,450 children in 378,390 cases.

I now turn to the description of the variables used in the analysis.

Outcome Variable

The outcome variable for this analysis is legal custody status, measured nominally with three possible categories: no custody, joint
custody, or sole custody. As noted above, legal custody may be different than the outcome for physical or residential custody. Legal custody
prescribes the rights granted to the parent with respect to decisions
affecting the child after the divorce. If the parties are legally married
prior to the birth of the child, both parents essentially have rights of
sole legal custody prior to divorce, that is, they may decide upon the
appropriate educational, medical, and religious aspects of a child's
upbringing. Moreover, both parents have access to the institutions that
provide for the educational, medical, and religious aspects of a child's
upbringing, as well as to information with respect to their child's
progress within these institutions. After divorce, one parent, in the
case of sole custody, has these rights, as do both parents in the case of
joint custody. Legal custody differs from physical custody in that legal
custody refers to the rights of parents to make decisions on behalf of
children, whereas physical custody refers to the actual living arrangements for the child. Sole or joint custody in this analysis refers only to
the determination of legal custodial status. Each parent-child relationship may achieve one of the three legal custodial statuses. For
example, if as a result of divorce the child is in the sole legal custody
of his or her mother, then the mother-child relation is assigned sole
legal custody status and the father-child relation is assigned no
custody status. If the child is in the joint legal custody of both parents,
both the father-child and mother-child relation are assigned joint legal
custody. If the child is assigned to the legal custody of someone other
than the mother or father, both parent-child relations are assigned no
legal custody status (see Table 2.1).

Independent Variables

The variation in custodial outcome can be explained by a number of
variables, all of which precede the custodial outcome in temporal
order. *Gender* is either male or female for each of the two parent-child
relations. *Petitioner* is the party who files for the divorce, that is, begins
the court action. The other party is referred to as the *respondent*.
Mothers in this sample were more than twice as frequently the petitioners as were fathers. Divorces in Canada can be decided upon with

Table 2.1 Custody assignment and legal custodial status

	Father-child relation	Mother-child relation
Sole custody to mother	No custody	Sole custody
Sole custody to father	Sole custody	No custody
Joint custody	Joint custody	Joint custody
Custody to other person or agency	No custody	No custody
No determination	No custody	No custody

the aid of a number of court hearings or without any hearing at all. When there is no hearing, the terms of the divorce may be negotiated with the assistance of mediators, or lawyers, or directly between the parties. The involvement of a legal hearing in a case can indicate both the agency of the individuals (litigiousness) and the structural effect produced by increased impingement of the legal system on the divorcing couple. The variable *hearing* indicates whether a hearing was held.

Since 1986, divorce in Canada can be granted on a number of different grounds, which are set out in the divorce petition. The variable *grounds* indicate the primary grounds cited for the divorce: separation for at least one year, adultery, physical cruelty, or mental cruelty. The *number of children* is the number of children for which a custody outcome is recorded for a given divorce. *Child's age at divorce* is measured in years and derived from the child's birth date and the date of divorce and is then divided into three categories: infants less than 2 years old, children (or dependents) over the age of 19, and all other children (between the ages of 2 and 19). *Family position* is categorized as: only child, and oldest, youngest, or middle child, depending on birth order. *Region* is Atlantic (New Brunswick, Nova Scotia, Prince Edward Island, or Newfoundland); Quebec; Ontario; Prairie (Manitoba, Saskatchewan, or Alberta); British Columbia; or North (Yukon, Northwest Territories, or Nunavut). *Time* is the number of years elapsed since 1986, the year of enactment of the most recent Canadian Divorce Act. *Marriage length* is the number of years from the marriage date until the date the divorce is officially granted. *Age difference* is the number of years that the husband is older than the wife. Age difference is negative if the wife is older than the husband. *Wife's age at marriage* is derived from the date of the marriage and the birth year of the wife. Note that this analysis is to some extent exploratory since the literature does not provide theoretical guidance on the prediction of the

Table 2.2 Frequency distributions of categorical variables

	Frequency	Per cent	Cumulative
Petitioner?			
No	733,999	54.50	54.50
Yes	612,901	45.50	100.00
Total	1,346,900	100.00	
Hearing?			
No	856,572	63.60	63.60
Yes	432,072	32.08	95.67
Missing	58,256	4.33	100.00
Total	1,346,900	100.00	
Primary grounds			
Separation	1,005,870	74.68	74.68
Adultery	86,266	6.40	81.09
Physical cruelty	5,198	0.39	81.47
Mental cruelty	65,390	4.85	86.33
Missing	184,176	13.67	100.00
Total	1,346,900	100.00	
Region			
Atlantic	144,274	10.71	10.71
Quebec	508,274	37.74	48.45
Ontario	178,698	13.27	61.72
Prairie	358,208	26.59	88.31
BC	152,332	11.31	99.62
North	5,114	0.38	100.0 0
Total	1,346,900	100	
Child's age group			
Infant (**<2**)	22,172	1.65	1.65
2-5 yrs	389,286	28.90	30.55
6-11 yrs	455,040	33.78	64.33
12-14 yrs	236,158	17.53	81.87
15-18 yrs	244,244	18.13	100.0 0
Total	1,346,900	100.00	
Family position			
Only child	312,300	23.19	23.19
Oldest	444,428	33.00	56.18
Middle	140,898	10.46	66.64
Youngest	449,274	33.36	100.00
Total	1,346,900	100.00	

Table 2.2 (*concluded*)

	Frequency	Per cent	Cumulative
Year			
1986	13,668	1.01	1.01
1987	79,486	5.9	6.92
1988	90,460	6.72	13.63
1989	91,484	6.79	20.42
1990	91,024	6.76	27.18
1991	94,962	7.05	34.23
1992	93,924	6.97	41.21
1993	93,954	6.98	48.18
1994	94,404	7.01	55.19
1995	93,664	6.95	62.14
1996	87,152	6.47	68.62
1997	78,016	5.79	74.41
1998	74,292	5.52	79.92
1999	75,340	5.59	85.52
2000	74,810	5.55	91.07
2001	71,620	5.32	96.39
2002*	48,640	3.61	100.0 0
Total	1,819,882	100.00	
No. of children			
1	312,300	23.19	23.19
2	669,382	49.7	72.88
3	274,950	20.41	93.3
4	70,770	5.25	98.55
5	12,446	0.92	99.48
6	4,918	0.37	99.84
7	1,010	0.07	99.92
8	664	0.05	99.97
9	186	0.01	99.98
10	184	0.01	99.99
11	66	0.00	100.00
12	24	0.00	100.00
Total	1,346,900	100	

*Includes data for the first nine months of 2002.

custody outcome for every variable under consideration. *Wife's age at divorce* is derived from the date of the divorce and the birth year of the wife. The age of the husband at marriage and divorce was not included in the model, along with the wife's age and the marriage length and age difference, since these ages can be derived from the other variables in the model.

Three more variables, called *interaction terms*, were also derived to indicate cases where the mother was accused of adultery, where the mother was involved in a hearing, and the length of the mother's marriage. This is to control for the historical differential effect on the mother's chances of custody where adultery is the primary ground for divorce, whether mothers see a decrease in chances for custody if there is a hearing, and to see if the legal construction of fatherhood through a relationship with the child's mother has an effect via the length of the marriage. Table 2.2 provides frequency distributions for categorical variables.

Method

The effects of the gender of the parent and a hearing on the custody outcome were first analysed using tables. Table-based techniques are limited when a large number of variables could affect the outcome under consideration, yet are worthwhile for the examining of important relationships. In order to assess the independent effects of each predictor on the outcome, multi-variate statistical modelling techniques were used. Two outcomes were modelled. The first was whether there was a hearing in the case (yes or no). An appropriate statistical model[8] was used to understand which variables predicted a greater likelihood of a hearing being held. The second was custody outcome, which had three possible values. A second statistical model[9] was used to assess the effects of predictors on the chances of gaining *joint* or *sole custody* as compared to *no custody*. Because the data used for this analysis contained a large number of cases, an alternative method for estimating the statistical significance of the effects of each independent variable was used, since conventional techniques may be biased to finding an effect when the number of cases is very large.

Results

A tabular analysis of the effect of the gender of the parent on custody determination suggests that the gender of the parent plays an important role in the determination of custody (see Table 2.3).

Women gain some form of custody 89 per cent of the time, while men completely lose custody in 67 per cent of cases. If you knew only

Table 2.3 Effect of parent's gender on custody outcome

| Custody | Gender of parent | | Total |
	Male	Female	
Sole	73,638 (11%)	449,042 (67%)	522,680 (39%)
Joint	149,375 (22%)	149,375 (22%)	298,750 (22%)
None	450,437 (67%)	75,033 (11%)	525,470 (39%)
Total	673,450 (100%)	673,450 (100%)	1,346,900 (100%)

the gender of the parent in all of these cases and no other information, you could predict the results correctly 78 per cent of the time. In other words, if you knew the parent was female you would guess she would get custody and be right 89 per cent of the time. Similarly, if the parent was male you would guess they would lose custody and be right in 67 per cent of cases; the average is 78 per cent. In terms of guessing the specific type of custody – joint, sole, or none – knowing the gender of the parent would allow you to guess correctly 67 per cent of the time. That is, if the parent was female you would guess she would be awarded sole custody and be accurate in 67 per cent of cases; if male you would guess he would get no custody and again be correct 67 per cent of the time.

Another measure of the predictive power of gender on custody is called the proportional reduction of errors (PRE). If you were guessing the outcome with no information on the case, you would guess *no custody*, since that is the most common outcome[10] and you would be right 39 per cent of the time and wrong 61 per cent of the time. If you knew the gender of the parent, you could make a better prediction of the specific custody outcome: if female you would guess *sole custody*, if male you would guess *no custody* and you would be right in 67 per cent of cases, reducing the errors from 61 to 33 per cent. This is a 46 per cent reduction in the errors if you know the gender of the parent. The PRE of gender when predicting the specific custody outcome is thus 46 per cent. However it is measured, the effect of the gender of the parent in custody outcomes is very large.

This result can be compared with a previous analysis by Prentice (1979:357) of custody data from 1975, as shown in Table 2.4.[11] This comparison would suggest that the (uncontrolled) effect of gender on custody has decreased in Canada since 1975; however, the removal of

Table 2.4 Effect of parent's gender on custody outcome (Prentice 1979, 1975 data)

Custody	Gender of parent		Total
	Male	Female	
Sole	3,552 (14%)	22,403 (86%)	25,955 (50%)
None	22,403 (86%)	3,552 (14%)	25,955 (50%)
Total	25,955 (100%)	25,955 (100%)	51,910 (100%)

Table 2.5 Effect of parent's gender on custody outcome (without joint custody)

Custody	Gender of parent		Total
	Male	Female	
Sole	73,638 (14%)	449,042 (86%)	522,680 (50%)
None	450,437 (86%)	75,033 (14%)	525,470 (50%)
Total	524,075 (100%)	524,075 (100%)	1,048,150 (100%)

Table 2.6 Effect of a hearing on custody outcome

Custody	Hearing		Total
	No hearing	Hearing	
Sole	312,528 (36%)	184,387 (43%)	496,915 (39%)
Joint	229,730 (27%)	62,396 (14%)	292,126 (22%)
None	314,314 (37%)	185,289 (43%)	499,603 (39%)
Total	856,572 (100%)	432,072 (100%)	1,288,644 (100%)

joint custody results from the current analysis provides a very similar result.

In other words, the decrease in the effect of gender from the mid-1970s seems to be due to the addition of the joint custody category, since, when this category is removed from the current analysis, results very similar to the previous analysis are obtained (see Table 2.5).

When it comes to the role of gender in sole custody, there has been no change since the mid-1970s, a surprising result given that an entirely rewritten divorce law was introduced at the federal level between the

Table 2.7 Effect of a hearing on custody outcome for mothers

Mothers	Hearing		Total
	No hearing	Hearing	
Sole	270,964 (63%)	156,477 (72%)	427,441 (67%)
Joint	114,865 (27%)	31,198 (14%)	146,063 (22%)
None	42,457 (10%)	28,361 (13%)	70,818 (11%)
Total	428,286 (100%)	216,036 (100%)	644,322 (100%)

Table 2.8 Effect of a hearing on custody outcome for fathers

Fathers	Hearing		Total
	No hearing	Hearing	
Sole	41,564 (10%)	27,910 (13%)	69,474 (11%)
Joint	114,865 (27%)	31,198 (14%)	146,063 (22%)
None	271,857 (63%)	156,928 (73%)	428,785 (67%)
Total	428,286 (100%)	216,036 (100%)	644,322 (100%)

two sets of data. So, when it comes to sole custody determinations in Canada, the gender of the parent has a very large effect on the outcome, an effect that is invariant over time, at least since the 1970s.

The bivariate relationship between a hearing and the custody outcome, in contrast, does not improve our ability to predict the custody outcome by much: the association is weak (see Table 2.6).

However, the chances of gaining sole custody are higher (43 per cent versus 36 per cent), and the chances of gaining joint custody are reduced by nearly half (from 27 to 14 per cent), when there is a hearing compared to when there is not. Although a hearing improves the chances of an outcome of sole custody, these probabilities are different depending on the gender of the parent. For example, a hearing improves the chances of gaining sole custody for both parents, but provides greater improvement for mothers, whose probability for sole custody is increased from 63 to 72 per cent (see Table 2.7).

On the other hand, a greater proportional increase is available to fathers, although their probabilities of winning sole custody are still only 13 per cent, or more than five times less than mothers (see Table 2.8).

Table 2.9 Effect of being the petitioner on custody outcome

	Legal role		
Custody	Respondent	Petitioner	Total
Sole	161,102 (22%)	361,578 (59%)	522,680 (39%)
Joint	168,584 (23%)	130,166 (21%)	298,750 (22%)
None	404,313 (55%)	121,157 (20%)	525,470 (39%)
Total	733,999 (100%)	612,901 (100%)	1,346,900 (100%)

Table 2.10 Effect of being the petitioner on custody outcome
(Prentice 1979, 1975 data)

	Legal role		
Custody	Respondent	Petitioner	Total
Sole	4,907 (19%)	21,048 (81%)	25,955 (50%)
None	21,048 (81%)	4,907 (19%)	25,955 (50%)
Total	25,955 (100%)	25,955 (100%)	51,910 (100%)

The uncontrolled effect of being the petitioner on the custody outcome is shown in Table 2.9. Before controlling for other variables, being the petitioner appears to increase the probability of gaining sole custody. Knowing whether the parent is the petitioner or the respondent allows the correct prediction of specific custody outcome in 57 per cent of cases. The petitioner gets some form of custody 80 per cent of the time, whereas the respondent only gets custody of some kind in 45 per cent of cases. We can also say that knowing the legal role of the parent reduces errors in predicting the custody outcome by 29 per cent, using the PRE measure described above.

This represents a change since the mid-1970s in Canada, when the effect of being the petitioner appeared to be greater: predicting the petitioner would gain custody reduced the errors in the prediction of custody by 62 per cent in that time period, when petitioners won custody in 81 per cent of cases (see Table 2.10). Even if the category of joint custody is removed from the current analysis, there still is a reduction since the mid-1970s in the effect of being the petitioner (knowing the legal role reduces errors predicting the custody result by 46 per cent).

The results, shown in Table 2.10, while providing some insight into the precursors of custody outcomes, do not account for the effects of other explanatory variables. In order to achieve this, statistical[12] models explaining variation in whether a hearing was held and the custody outcome were constructed.

Model of Whether a Hearing Was Held

The model explaining *whether* a hearing was held provides some insight as to *why* there is variation in whether a hearing was held (see Appendix A (p. 35) for the numerical results from the models discussed below). This model shows that there is great regional disparity in the use of hearings, with cases in Quebec having roughly 10 times the odds of involving a hearing than in the Prairie region, and more than 4 times that of Ontario. Moreover, there is a very strong trend over time against the use of hearings in the course of a divorce, with a 16 per cent reduction in the odds of a hearing in a case for every year after 1986. With respect to the grounds for divorce, physical cruelty claims were the most likely to involve a hearing, whereas mental cruelty grounds were the least likely, this perhaps related to the quality of evidence available for presentation in court. Mothers and respondents are slightly less likely than fathers and petitioners to be involved in a hearing, even though each case involves a mother and a father and a petitioner (or plaintiff) and a respondent, due to the shared variation of these variables with others in the model. The longer the marriage, the less likely the divorce will involve a hearing. For each additional child in the family, there is an expected 5 per cent increase in the odds a hearing will be involved in the divorce. Children 15 years of age and over are less likely to be involved in a hearing, a finding that may be due to the ability of older children to have their choice of living arrangements recognized by the courts. The model correctly predicts whether there was a hearing 70 per cent of the time, and reduces the errors of prediction by 29.5 per cent compared to guessing that there was no hearing (the most common situation).

Model of Custody Awards

The models explaining variation in the custody outcome were performed first without, and then with, the three interaction terms[13] with the gender of the parent. The first model, with no interaction effects included, highlights the strong effect of the gender of the parent in determining the custody outcome. For example, mothers – compared to fathers – are approximately 27 times (2,600 per cent) more likely to obtain sole custody than no custody, and have more than 5 times the odds of achieving joint custody over no custody. There also appears to be an important advantage in being the petitioner or initiator of the divorce action: being the petitioner increased the odds of obtaining both joint and sole custody over no custody by 71 per cent and 281 per cent, respectively, perhaps since petitioners are also usually the initiators of the relationship dissolution and have the advantage of surprise and greater motivation to see the legal process through. Regional differences, again with Quebec and the Prairies on opposite ends of the spectrum, are also apparent. Quebec is the province least likely to order a child into joint custody and the most likely to order sole custody, compared to no custody. The regional differences are highest for joint custody, with the regions varying only slightly in the relative odds for sole custody. The Prairie region is about two and a half times more likely than Ontario to order joint custody, while Quebec has about two-thirds the odds of a joint custody outcome as Ontario. British Columbia and the Atlantic region are also more likely to order joint custody than is Ontario.

With respect to grounds for divorce, separation of at least a year was found to increase the chances of both joint and sole custody. In particular, both physical and mental cruelty claims appear to reduce the chances of joint custody significantly. For each additional year of marriage, there is an expected increase in the odds of receiving joint custody over no custody, controlling for the other variables in the model, but no effect on the odds of gaining sole custody. For each additional child in the family there is an expected decrease of 17 per cent in the odds of receiving joint custody, controlling for the other variables in the model, along with a decrease of 2 per cent in the odds of gaining sole custody, compared to no custody. A child's age and family position had only small effects on the likelihood of sole custody; however, pre-school children were associated with increased odds of joint custody, while an 'only' child was less likely to end up in joint custody of both his or her parents. There was a pronounced trend over time towards orders of joint custody: a 14 per cent increase in the odds of this custodial status per year, controlling for the other variables in the model, while there was only a very slight increase in the odds of an order of sole custody over time (0.3 per cent). Spouses who were similar in age had a greater likelihood of achieving joint custody than did couples who differed in age by more than five years. Wives who were significantly older than their husbands had worse chances of gaining joint custody than did husbands who were older than their wives. Longer marriages increased the odds of joint custody, with a 6 per cent expected increase in the odds of joint custody for each additional year of marriage. The wife's age at marriage or divorce had no effect on the likelihood of either joint or sole custody. This model (without interactions) reduces the errors in the prediction of the custody outcomes by 47.8 per cent, and correctly predicts the custody outcome 68 per cent of the time.

A second model of custody outcomes tested to see if there were effects from the interaction of gender with length of marriage, grounds of adultery, and whether a hearing was held. The length of marriage was theorized to interact with gender, since the legal role of father is legally constructed indirectly through the relationship with the child's mother. That is, the biological or social connection of a man with his child is less relevant from a legal perspective than the relationship of the man with the child's mother. To test the potential effect of this legal construction of the paternal relationship, an interaction term of gender by length of marriage was added to the model.

Another potential factor in the awarding of custody is the historic double standard applied to women with respect to adultery. For example, the early custody laws discussed above granted a mother rights to custody of her children, but only if she had not committed adultery, a caveat not applied to men. An interaction term of gender with cases where the primary ground of adultery was cited in the petition for divorce was added to test the continued existence of this historic prejudice. A third interaction term was added to test for the effect that a hearing has a differential effect vis-à-vis gender.

The gender interaction terms in this model all decrease the odds of both joint and sole custody, that is, they operate in the opposite direction of gender. This has the consequence of making the effects much higher for the parent's gender than the previous model, with no interaction terms, with mothers (compared to fathers) having about 142 times greater odds of achieving sole custody and 12 times greater odds of achieving joint custody compared to no custody when there is no hearing, the husband has not filed on the basis of adultery, and when the marriage is very short. In cases where the husband has alleged adultery on the part of the wife, the odds of the wife achieving joint or sole custody are reduced by 37 and 58 per cent, respectively. The longer a wife is married, the less her chances of custody, with the odds of gaining joint custody reduced by 5 per cent and the odds of gaining sole custody reduced by 10 per cent for each year of marriage, controlling for the other variables in the model. Hearings also reduce the chances of wives gaining custody by 8 and 16 per cent for joint and sole custody, respectively.

Discussion

This analysis examines the precursors to hearings and custody outcomes in Canadian divorce cases. The sample includes the complete data of divorces granted from 1 June 1986 until September 2002 under Canada's second Divorce Act, involving the custody determinations of more than 650,000 children over the age of one year. The most prominent finding related to custody determinations is the primary role of gender in the production of custody outcomes. The influence of gender is enormous, increasing the odds of mothers obtaining sole custody by more than 27 times and the odds of mothers obtaining joint custody by more than 5 times, compared to not obtaining some form of legal custody. While this effect for gender is powerful, there appear to be conflicting forces at play. The dominant of these favours women; however, there are several gender-related factors that act against the likelihood of a mother obtaining custody. For example, the longer a father is married to the children's mother, the greater the chance he will obtain custody (or the less likely the mother will), since the legal definitions of fatherhood are largely based on the father's relationship with the mother as opposed to his relationship with the child. In addition, the traditional stigma with respect to adultery appears to have an effect, as well, to women's disadvantage. Moreover, if a case involves a hearing, women's chances for custody are reduced, an effect noticed elsewhere. If these mitigating factors (adultery, marriage length, and a hearing) were not present, the chances of a mother gaining custody would be even higher than the 2,600 per cent advantage for mothers.

The official standard for custody determination, as provided by the Divorce Act of 1986, is the 'best interests of the child.' Thus, one might argue that parenting abilities or other qualities that are considered to be in the best interests of children are highly correlated with gender, and that it is these parenting skills or other qualities that are determinative and not gender per se. This is a question that will be addressed in more detail later in this work. A finding of such a drastic difference in outcomes by gender in virtually any other field of human endeavour would almost certainly lead to strong suspicions of gender bias. Nevertheless, it is possible that variables having unmeasured covariation with gender or with other variables in the model variables that *do* relate to the best interests of children have an effect. For example, it is important to assess whether gender differences in caregiving or other characteristics result in important differentials in outcomes for children, and this question will be pursued in the next chapter. The models presented in this study suggest that more than two-thirds of the custody outcomes can be predicted by the variables in the model, all of which precede the custody outcome in time. Since a large amount of the variation in custody can be explained with variables that are not usually strongly associated with children's 'best interests,' the question of whether the variables of the model share variance with variables that are related to beneficial outcomes for children becomes more important.

The results for the interaction of gender and the involvement of a legal hearing are consistent with a well-known study on the custody assignment process conducted by Maccoby and Mnookin (1992). In that study, fathers were slightly more likely to achieve custody if they took the case to court, as is the case here; however, they were most commonly motivated to pursue legal custody because of concerns about the children's welfare while in the care of the mother. As in this case, while the fathers had increased chances of custody in the Maccoby and Mnookin study, the courts nonetheless granted custody to mothers many times more often than to fathers. We cannot comment here on the motivation for greater legal involvement from the point of view of either party, yet it would seem consistent with these results that fathers would be unlikely to brave very poor odds unless motivated by an issue that was pressing from their point of view.

There were several other interesting findings offered by these models. For example, there is large regional variation in the use of both hearings and joint custody, but little variation in the ordering of sole custody by region. Joint custody is a steadily increasing outcome for all regions over time, perhaps reflecting an attempt by the legal system to move towards gender equality. However, a joint legal custody outcome is more likely to be a conventional sole residential custody to the mother, with some rights to information for the father, than a truly equal outcome. The advantage to the petitioner is interesting, since

there is no substantive legal reason for this. It could be that the petitioner has an element of surprise, with the respondent scrambling to
understand his or her legal rights, obtain counsel, and formulate a
legal strategy. It could also suggest that the person initiating the
divorce does so because they have an advantage, that is, the petitioner
waits until an opportune time to file for divorce. A hearing appears to
decrease the chance of joint custody by about 10 per cent, but only
slightly increases the odds of obtaining sole custody. Thus, the
impingement of the courts on the custody determination process
mainly affects the rate of joint custody, perhaps because 'bargaining in
the shadow of the law' produces similar custody results. The reduced
odds of obtaining joint custody are most likely explained by the presence of increased conflict or litigiousness, rather than by a structural
effect of a hearing.

The most important predictors for a hearing are the region in which
the divorce takes place and whether or not the divorce petition alleges
physical abuse. Physical abuse might affect whether a hearing takes
place simply because evidence of physical abuse is generally easier to
demonstrate than other kinds of mistreatment. The likelihood of a
hearing also increases when the husband is more than five years older
than the wife.

Conditions of the marriage have a bearing on both the involvement
of a legal hearing and the custody outcome. Longer marriages are less
likely to involve a hearing, and are more likely to involve a custody
award. The longer a marriage, the more the mother loses some of her
advantage in gaining custody, reflecting the legal construction of the
father's relation to his children. The claim of divorce on the traditionally stigmatic ground of adultery also reduces a mother's odds of
being granted either joint or sole custody. Thus, there is evidence of the
vestiges of traditional (double) standards of marital behaviour
expected of women on the custody outcome. Large differences in age
between the divorcing parties decrease the possibility of joint custody,
compared to the other possible custodial outcomes. However, the age
of the mother appears to have no effect on the custodial outcome.

Overall, the results of this analysis suggest that traditional ideas
about gender roles and marital behaviour appear to dominate the
process of custody assignment. The theory of bargaining in the
'shadow of the law,' that is, that negotiations conducted without legal
involvement do not differ substantially from those arrived at with the
assistance of legal venues, is largely supported. For example, the like-

lihood of a sole custody order is the same whether there is a hearing or not. However, some differences do arise: joint custody is less likely if a legal hearing is accessed, and mothers have a slightly worse chance of achieving custody if there is a hearing in the case. These differences likely reflect differences in the individuals, rather than a structural effect from a hearing and the fact that the movement into the legal arena is not without barriers. Invoking court hearings involves significant investments, not only financially, although these can be substantial, but also in time and the inevitable emotional toll that the additional conflict will bring. Thus, it is to be expected that the parties involved might tolerate small variations from the legal regime because they are not worth the trouble required to achieve them, even if they are not in that party's favour. Nonetheless, the presence of large variations in custody outcome by region suggests that the outcome in court has a powerful effect on the outcomes negotiated in its shadow, as predicted by the legal realism perspective. It follows that if change is desired in how custody decisions are arrived at, it must start with the courts since the expected result in court is highly determinative to agreements negotiated out of court.

APPENDIX A

Preparation of the Data

The data were provided in a series of three files, each containing a table: a master table that contained one record for each divorce; another table containing one record per court; and a third table with one record per child of divorce. The children file contains only children involved in a divorce processed under Canada's second Divorce Act, proclaimed in effect as of 1 June 1986. Thus, although many of the divorces present in the master table involved the custody of children, the details of the ages of these children are not present in the data available for analysis. These three files are related, as shown in Figure A.1. The first table contained information about the divorce case, such as the characteristics of the parties, date the divorce was granted, and whether there was a formal hearing involved in the divorce process. The second table contained information on the birth date and the custody award disposition for each child involved in a divorce. The third table was a list of all courts in Canada, with a description that

Figure A.1: Relationships of original files

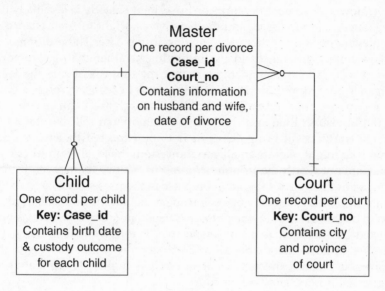

included the city and province in which they are located. This table was manipulated with Microsoft Excel to extract the city and province as separate fields from the description. These three tables were translated from the plain text format with which they were provided into a format suitable for use by the statistical program Stata. The files were first processed individually, creating derived variables, labelling all variables, and generating a codebook for each table or file. Table A.1 shows the number of records and the number of derived variables for each original file.

The derived variables from the master file included variables that translated the text forms of dates into Stata's internal (numerical) date format and variables requiring the calculation of differences between dates, such as the ages of the husband and wife at marriage and divorce. The derived variables from the child table included the number of children in the family, the birth order, an indicator for multiple births, and the family position of the child. The number of children involved in each divorce was calculated by counting the number of children in each divorce. The birth order of each child within a given family was derived using the child's birth date. Twins or multiple birth children were arbitrarily ordered since their birth dates were the same,

Table A1 Contents of files

Table	Records	Original variables	Derived variables	Total variables
Master	2,554,271	14	12	26
Child	705,684	3	9	12
Court	228	7	0	7

but were flagged as multiple births. The birth order and the number of children in the family were then used to classify each child as either an only child, or alternatively as the oldest, youngest, or middle child. Since the data are expected to be released to the general public for further research, the variables were not necessarily created with the intent of using them in this analysis. Instead, the approach taken was to create as many variables as possible, as many as might be used in further analyses.

Since this analysis involved the custody of children, the data from the child table were connected to the master and court tables, resulting in a single file containing 56 variables (43 from the original files and 13 derived variables) on 705,684 children of divorce in 399,474 cases in Canada, including information on the child, the divorce, and the court involved. The derived variables included the child's age and age group at divorce.

There are several units of analysis that could be used for analysis of these data: the divorce, the child, and the parent-child relation. Since the research question here involves the determination of child custody, the parent-child relation was chosen as the unit of analysis. This allows comparison between the father-child and mother-child relation to determine which characteristics of each relation (if any) might influence the custody outcome. To create a file with the parent-child relation as the unit of analysis, two records were created for each child involved in a divorce, resulting in a file with 1,411,368 records. Each of these records contained the information related to both the case and the child, one for the father and one for the mother. Since same-sex marriages have only recently been legalized by some jurisdictions in Canada, and indeed have not yet been federally recognized at the time of writing, it is assumed that all divorces involved one man and one woman, additionally assumed to be the father and mother in the relationship with the child. Thus, the legal definition of parent is used as

Table A2 Allowable ranges for variables

Variable (x)	Range	Comments
Age difference	$-30 \geq x \leq 36$	Average age difference is approximately 3 years.
Child's age at divorce	$1 \geq x \leq 19$	Infants less than 1 year were excluded to avoid the issue of breastfeeding.
Wife's age at divorce	$19 \geq x \leq 65$	
Husband's age at divorce	$19 \geq x \leq 65$	
Number of children	$1 \geq x \leq 12$	Two cases had more than 12 children
Length of marriage (years)	$1 \geq x \leq 45$	
Wife's age at marriage	$16 \geq x \leq 50$	
Husband's age at marriage	$16 \geq x \leq 65$	
Divorce disposition code	$x = 4$	Divorce granted
Date of divorce	> 01 June 1986	Divorce law changed effective this date

opposed to the biological definition; that is, any children defined as 'children of the marriage,' be they adopted or acquired in any other fashion, are included in the analysis. Variables were created to indicate the gender of the parent and whether sole or joint custody was obtained as the outcome of the divorce.

After removing 64,468, or 4.5 per cent, of records containing data that seemed potentially miscoded or otherwise unreliable (see Table A.2 for a list of criteria used to verify data), 1,346,900 records representing 673,450 children in 378,390 cases remained available for analysis.

Table A3 Logistic regression on whether a hearing was held

Variable	Categories	Odds ratio	Coefficient	Probability	
Gender	Mother? (1=yes)	0.97	-0.03	0.000	***
Legal role	Petitioner? (1=yes)	1.08	0.07	0.000	***
Grounds	Separation (ref.)				
	Adultery	1.02	0.02	0.318	
	Physical cruelty	1.46	0.38	0.000	***
	Mental cruelty	1.01	0.01	0.662	
Family size	Number of children	1.05	0.05	0.000	***
Age of child	Pre-school 2-5 yrs (ref.)				
	Infant <2 yrs	1.03	0.03	0.226	
	Elem. school 6-11 yrs.	1.02	0.02	0.105	
	Jr. high 12-14 yrs.	1.00	0.00	0.810	
	Sr. high 15-18 yrs.	0.96	-0.05	0.011	*
Family position	Only child (ref.)				
	Oldest	0.97	-0.04	0.036	*
	Middle	0.95	-0.05	0.016	*
	Youngest	0.96	-0.05	0.006	**
Region	Ontario (ref.)				
	Atlantic	1.88	0.63	0.000	***
	Quebec	4.41	1.48	0.000	***
	Prairie	0.43	-0.84	0.000	***
	B.C.	0.55	-0.59	0.000	***
	North	0.25	-1.39	0.000	***
Time	Years after 1986	0.84	-0.17	0.000	***
Duration	Length of marriage	0.93	-0.08	0.000	
Age difference	Similar ages (ref.)				
	Wife >5 years older	0.80	-0.23	0.340	
		0.86	-0.15	0.112	
		0.98	-0.02	0.601	
		1.03	0.03	0.028	*
		1.08	0.07	0.002	**
	Husb. >5 years older	1.11	0.11	0.006	**
Wife's age	at marriage	0.93	-0.07	0.000	***
	at divorce	1.08	0.08	0.000	***
	N	1,106,326			
	Pseudo R2, PRE	18.4%	29.5%		
	*p<.05; **p<.01;*** p<.001 (two tailed)				

PRE=Proportional Reduction in Error in predicting the dependent variable.
This model predicts the variable 'hearing' correctly 70 per cent of the time.

Table A4 Multinominal regression on custodial outcome (no interactions)

Variable	Categories	Joint custody			Sole custody		
		Odds ratio	Coefficient	Prob.	Odds ratio	Coefficient	Prob.
Gender	Mother? (1=yes)	5.37	1.68	0.000 ***	27.42	3.31	0.000 ***
Legal role	Petitioner? (1=yes)	1.71	0.54	0.000 ***	3.81	1.34	0.000 ***
Legality	Hearing? (1=yes)	0.89	-0.11	0.000 ***	0.97	-0.03	0.000 ***
Grounds	Separation (ref.)						
	Adultery	0.89	-0.12	0.000 ***	0.85	-0.16	0.000 ***
	Physical cruelty	0.47	-0.76	0.000 ***	0.89	-0.12	0.000 ***
	Mental cruelty	0.55	-0.59	0.000 ***	0.85	-0.16	0.000 ***
Family size	Number of children	0.83	-0.19	0.000 ***	0.98	-0.02	0.000 ***
Age of child	Preschool 2-5 yrs (ref.)						
	Infant (<2 yrs)	0.61	-0.49	0.000 ***	1.01	0.01	0.018 *
	Elem. school (6-11 yrs)	0.95	-0.05	0.000 ***	1.00	0.00	0.006 **
	Jr. high (12-14 yrs)	0.78	-0.25	0.000 ***	0.99	-0.01	0.000 ***
	High school (15-18)	0.60	-0.50	0.000 ***	0.99	-0.01	0.000 ***
Child situation	Only child (ref.)						
	Oldest	1.58	0.45	0.000 ***	1.01	0.01	0.000 ***
	Middle	1.47	0.39	0.000 ***	1.01	0.01	0.000 ***
	Youngest	1.40	0.33	0.000 ***	1.01	0.01	0.000 ***
Region	Ontario (ref.)						
	Atlantic	1.43	0.36	0.000 ***	1.00	0.00	0.158
	Quebec	0.66	-0.42	0.000 ***	1.19	0.17	0.000 ***
	Prairie	2.53	0.93	0.000 ***	0.97	-0.03	0.000 ***
	B.C.	1.55	0.44	0.000 ***	1.00	0.00	0.055
	North	2.58	0.95	0.000 ***	0.97	-0.03	0.000 ***

Table A4 (continued)

Variable	Categories	Joint custody			Sole custody		
		Odds ratio	Coefficient	Prob.	Odds ratio	Coefficient	Prob.
Time	Years after 1986	1.14	0.13	0.000 ***	1.00	0.00	0.000 ***
Duration	Length of marriage	1.06	0.06	0.000 ***	1.00	0.00	0.088
Age difference	Similar ages (ref.)						
	Wife 15+ years older	0.43	-0.85	0.016 *	0.93	-0.07	0.009 **
	Wife 10-14 years older	0.60	-0.52	0.000 ***	0.98	-0.02	0.003 **
	Wife 5-9 years older	0.59	-0.53	0.000 ***	0.98	-0.02	0.000 ***
	Husb. 5-9 years older	0.93	-0.07	0.000 ***	0.99	-0.01	0.000 ***
	Husb. 10-14 years older	0.82	-0.20	0.000 ***	0.98	-0.02	0.000 ***
	Husb. 15+ years older	0.71	-0.34	0.000 ***	0.97	-0.03	0.000 ***
Wife's age	At marriage	1.02	0.02	0.061	1.00	0.00	0.671
	At divorce	1.00	0.00	0.735	1.00	0.00	0.929
	N	1,579,370					
	Pseudo R2, PRE	27.8%	47.8%				

*p<.05; **p<.01;*** p<.001 (two tailed)

PRE=Proportional Reduction in Error in predicting the dependent variable.
This model predicts the custody outcome correctly 68 per cent of the time.

Table A5 Multinominal regression on custodial outcome (with interactions)

Variable	Categories	Joint custody			Sole custody		
		Odds ratio	Coefficient	Prob.	Odds ratio	Coefficient	Prob.
Gender	Mother? (1=yes)	12.34	2.51	0.000 ***	142.61	4.96	0.000 ***
Legal role	Petitioner? (1=yes)	1.68	0.52	0.000 ***	3.67	1.30	0.000 ***
Legality	Hearing? (1=yes)	0.90	-0.10	0.000 ***	1.07	0.06	0.000 ***
Grounds	Separation (ref.)						
	Adultery	0.97	-0.03	0.217	1.31	0.27	0.000 ***
	Physical cruelty	0.47	-0.76	0.000 ***	0.88	-0.12	0.000 ***
	Mental cruelty	0.55	-0.59	0.000 ***	0.85	-0.16	0.000 ***
Family size	Number of children	0.83	-0.19	0.000 ***	0.98	-0.02	0.000 ***
Age of child	Preschool 2-5 yrs (ref.)						
	Infant (<2 yrs)	0.62	-0.48	0.000 ***	1.01	0.01	0.133
	Elem. school (6-11 yrs)	0.95	-0.06	0.000 ***	1.00	0.00	0.131
	Jr. high (12-14 yrs)	0.78	-0.25	0.000 ***	0.99	-0.01	0.005 **
	High school (15-18)	0.60	-0.50	0.000 ***	0.99	-0.01	0.000 ***
Child situation	Only child (ref.)						
	Oldest	1.57	0.45	0.000 ***	1.01	0.01	0.000 ***
	Middle	1.47	0.38	0.000 ***	1.01	0.01	0.000 ***
	Youngest	1.39	0.33	0.000 ***	1.01	0.01	0.000 ***
Region	Ontario (ref.)						
	Atlantic	1.43	0.36	0.000 ***	1.00	0.00	0.303
	Quebec	0.66	-0.42	0.000 ***	1.19	0.17	0.000 ***
	Prairie	2.53	0.93	0.000 ***	0.97	-0.03	0.000 ***
	B.C.	1.55	0.44	0.000 ***	1.00	0.00	0.027 *
	North	2.58	0.95	0.000 ***	0.97	-0.03	0.000 ***

Table A5 (continued)

Variable	Categories	Joint custody			Sole custody		
		Odds ratio	Coefficient	Prob.	Odds ratio	Coefficient	Prob.
Time	Years after 1986	1.14	0.13	0.000 ***	1.00	0.00	0.000 ***
Duration	Length of marriage	1.07	0.07	0.000 ***	1.06	0.06	0.000 ***
Age difference	Similar ages (ref.)						
	Wife 15+ years older	0.43	-0.86	0.016 *	0.94	-0.06	0.018 *
	Wife 10-14 years older	0.59	-0.52	0.000 ***	0.98	-0.02	0.007 **
	Wife 5-9 years older	0.59	-0.53	0.000 ***	0.98	-0.02	0.000 ***
	Husb. 5-9 years older	0.93	-0.07	0.000 ***	0.99	-0.01	0.000 ***
	Husb. 10-14 years older	0.82	-0.20	0.000 ***	0.98	-0.02	0.000 ***
	Husb. 15+ years older	0.71	-0.34	0.000 ***	0.97	-0.03	0.000 ***
Wife's age	At marriage	1.02	0.02	0.058	1.00	0.00	0.635
	At divorce	1.00	0.00	0.723	1.00	0.00	0.984
Interactions with gender	Marriage length	0.95	-0.05	0.000 ***	0.90	-0.11	0.000 ***
	Grounds of adultery	0.63	-0.46	0.000 ***	0.42	-0.87	0.000 ***
	Hearing	0.92	-0.09	0.000 ***	0.84	-0.18	0.000 ***
N		1,106,326					
Pseudo R2, PRE		28.3%	47.8%				

*p<.05; **p<.01;*** p<.001 (two tailed)

PRE=Proportional Reduction in Error in predicting the dependent variable.
This model predicts the custody outcome correctly 68 per cent of the time.

3 Explaining Children's Outcomes in the Context of Their Families

The legal framework which produced the results from the previous chapter is premised on a search for the best interests of the child. Since those results are very strongly correlated with gender, I will review what various theoretical perspectives claim *are* in children's best interests to see the weight given to gender – or characteristics strongly associated with gender – as a criterion for custody, along with other factors that stakeholders in the custody decision-making process deem appropriate to use in making their decisions. By stakeholders, I mean professionals that affect the custody decision-making process, such as judges, lawyers, and custody evaluators. In this chapter I review the literature with respect to the theoretical perspectives offered by social theory, such as James Coleman's social capital perspective, and discuss possible causal linkages that explain how the adjustment of children is affected by divorce, family configurations, and parenting. In this way I hope to highlight and contrast the factors considered important for children as presented by the major theoretical perspectives, and ultimately to form a model suitable for empirical testing that will explain variations in children's behavioural, health, and educational outcomes. I expect to use the family as the primary explanatory context, since choosing between different family configurations is the major issue in any custody determination. Ideally, the perspectives used by custody evaluators and legal actors, as well as by researchers on children, may be informed by the results of the empirical test of theory provided here.

The previous chapter illustrated the enormous influence that parental gender has on custody determinations in Canada; however, it may be that the relationship of gender with custody outcome is explained by other factors theoretically relevant to the best interests of the child, such as parenting that could be strongly correlated with gender and justify the apparent reliance on that characteristic. A central question of this work is, then: to what extent does the gender of a child's caregiver relate to attributes that are demonstrably in the child's interest? The answer is of some importance in the light of constitutional protections against reliance on gender for the decisions of public institutions such as the justice system, and the historical disadvantage fathers have faced when attempting to retain custody of their children.

The chapter begins with a review of some theoretical concepts relevant to the discussion, including ideas about social capital, legal and psychological paradigms regarding custody evaluation, as well as the resiliency of children, in preparation for the formation of a model for empirical testing. Subsequent chapters will deal with the methods used in performing the empirical tests and the results of those tests.

I now begin with a review of orienting concepts that frame the analysis. The section immediately following reviews the ways in which the parental relationship is theoretically an asset to the child, and how, in this formulation, divorce affects children.

Social Capital and the Parental Relationship

In order to theorize about how changes in social relations and especially family relationships – divorce, separation, and marriage – affect children, the concept of social capital is introduced. While *economic capital* consists of tangible resources and *human capital* rests in human skills and knowledge (usually acquired through education and experience), both of which can be used to facilitate production, *social capital* lies in the relations among people that facilitate action. Human capital can make use of tangible assets – economic capital – to increase production. Social capital, like human and economic capital, is 'productive, making possible the achievement of certain ends that in its absence would not be possible' (Coleman 1988:S98). Coleman (1987) defines social capital in the raising of children as 'the norms, the social networks, and the relationships between adults and children that are of value for the child's growing up. Social capital exists within the family, but also outside the family in the community' (36). However, for the purposes of this study, it is family and specifically parent-child relationships that are of interest, since custody decisions inevitably involve choosing among them. Coleman (1990) elaborates that social capital within the family has three important aspects: the parent-child relationship, the parent-parent relationship, and the continuity of the parent-parent relationship (590). Social capital thus emphasizes the importance of human networks and relationships for children, both in quantity and quality. The quality of relationships varies according to characteristics such as the trust and positive expectations in those relationships, maintained by parenting practices. Social capital can have both positive and negative aspects, since not all social relationships are positive and most relations contain both positive and negative aspects: relationships both support and constrain the individuals involved (Portes 1998).

Since children are born without human capital, the acquisition of skills and knowledge required for success in the adult world is achieved though relations with others, that is, social capital. Social capital is related to social control in that informal social control is accomplished through relations with socially proximate actors, which for children are, first, parents, then other caregivers, teachers, family members, and peers. For the purposes of this study, the parental relationship will be the most important consideration, since custody determinations are usually related to deciding how to reconfigure parental relationships after divorce. Formal social control, therefore, affects the relationships available after divorce, which in turn informally provides or removes social capital for the developing child. Children in North American society are provided fewer and fewer available supportive adult relationships, since the presence of extended family members in the household is becoming increasingly rare. Hence, for children, the quantity and quality of the social capital that remains is crucial for their development. Social capital theory, then, suggests that establishing and maintaining high-quality supportive relationships is in children's best interests.

It should not be surprising, under this framework, that social science studies have documented elevated levels of negative outcomes for children of divorce, compared to other children (Cherlin et al. 1991; Ely et al. 1999; Furstenberg 1990), since divorce frequently involves the downgrading of at least one of the parental relationships. The challenge of family law is how to structure family relationships so that children's life chances are maximized: the focus for custody decisions will usually be on the quality of the parental relationship, since the family structure has already dissolved. The focus at birth needs to be on the available parental figures and how to connect them in a way that enables these adults to be resources (social capital) to the child. The legal framework around birth, however, only connects the child to her or his mother, with the connection to the father(s) contingent on the relationship to the mother. I refer to fathers in the plural because in a significant minority of cases, the social, legal, and biological fathers are not necessarily the same person. All of these may have a potential impact on the child. Since the law already bestows custody based on a social relationship via the child's mother, the possibility of benefits arising from a biological father are relevant for consideration, even when a social father is involved with the child. These benefits can be categorized as financial support, health management benefits, psychosocial benefits, and legal rights. With respect to financial support, there are already precedents where a woman bore a child from a man who was not her spouse. In one such case, the court connected the child to both fathers, by recognizing the spouse of the woman as a guardian of the child while ordering child support from the biological father (Keller v. MacDonald 1998). In another case, a biological father described as a sperm donor by the mother was granted access to the child, allowing the child to receive instrumental support from the biological father (Johnson-Steeves v. Lee 1997). Where the biological father of the child is not correctly identified, or where the law does not enable the connection between father and child, the child could be missing out on financial or instrumental support that would otherwise be available.

With respect to health management, the biological heritage of an individual is one of the most important tools at her or his disposal. Accordingly, a study of the opinions of geneticists found that 70 per cent were in favour of adopted children being given the right to know the complete medical history of their biological parents (Lisker et al. 1998). It seems less than adequate not to accord non-adopted children the same right. The knowledge of one's genetic heritage provides information on exposure to genetic conditions and predispositions that may have great import on health management. For example, a genetic condition known as hemochromatosis may be carried by as many as 14 per cent of Caucasians and be present in about half a per cent (Olnyk et al. 1999). This condition can cause organ damage or even death if left untreated, yet treatment is simple and effective if the condition is correctly diagnosed in time. This is but one of many genetic conditions; others include familial hypercholesterolemia, polycystic kidney disease, Huntington's chorea, von Willebrand disease, achondroplaseia, sickle-cell anaemia, cystic fibrosis, Tay-Sachs disease, phenylketonuria, and mucopolysacchridoses, among others.

The biological status of one's parents is one of the most important predictors of a person's future health (Lisker et al. 1998), not only in terms of knowledge of genetic conditions, but also with respect to health risks over the life course. Yet some children, by the circumstances of their birth, do not have knowledge of their biological heritage. This is due not only to the legal framework but also to de facto medical policy about disclosing paternity issues. When mistaken paternity is discovered by a health professional, medical textbooks advise non-disclosure or disclosure only to the mother (Leikin 1995; Novitski 1977). Nearly all geneticists follow this policy, and many would go further and lie about the results if questioned (Lisker et al. 1998; Wertz, Fletcher, and Mulvihill 1990), even though as geneticists they are aware of the health benefits to the child of knowing her or his genetic heritage. Some psychological and social aspects of the developing person are also predicated on knowing one's biological heritage, such as family medical history, genealogy, and cultural and religious background (Pearson and Thoennes 1996). The knowledge of one's parents is also important for identity formation: children who have correct information are in a better position in this regard than are children who are not. In addition to financial health and psychological benefits, there are important legal rights that are based on one's biological parentage, such as the right to inherit and the right to citizenship (Hirczy 2000). Some of these rights are derived from statute and common law, but they also find support from the United Nations Convention on the Rights of the Child (Detrick 1992):

Article 7
1. The child shall be registered immediately after birth and shall have the right from birth to a name, the right to acquire a nationality and. as far as possible, the right to know and be cared for by his or her parents.
...
Article 8
1. States Parties undertake to respect the right of the child to preserve his or her identity, including nationality, name and family relations as recognized by law without unlawful interference.

Regardless of the source of the legal policy, a child-centred approach to legal decision-making should lean towards connecting children to as many adult resources early in life as is practicable. Mistaken paternal identity is common enough among divorcing couples to warrant some consideration when formulating judicial policy. A study of 7,867 DNA paternity tests in Canada undertaken for child support purposes revealed that 23 per cent of the putative fathers were incorrectly identified (Millar 2001). While this rate is likely higher than that for all divorcing couples, it indicates a prevalence that is substantial. The benefits to the child of knowing his or her father and the prevalence of non-paternity make it an issue of some import in divorce.

I now examine social science evidence with respect to the mechanisms of how divorce affects children through changes in family structure and through the divorce process itself.

Family Structure and the Process of Divorce

One of the most universally reported findings in social science is that children of intact two-parent families fare better than do children of other family forms in terms of behavioural, health, and educational outcomes (Cherlin et al. 1991; Ely et al. 1999; Mauldon 1990). Moreover, the effects of divorce on children may be long term, affecting adult relationships of children who grew up in divorced families (Amato and Sobolewski 2001; Furstenberg, Hoffman, and Shrestha 1995). Deficits associated with divorce are measurable in virtually all aspects of children's lives, including health, behavioural (including delinquency), and educational or cognitive outcomes. For example, Mauldon (1990) found that divorce was a strong risk factor for illness in children, even after controlling for a wide range of other factors. Furstenberg and Hughes (1995) found that children in families where the biological father was present were four times more likely to complete high school. Cherlin et al. (1991) examined more than 11,000 children in the U.K. and found that both parent- and teacher-reported behaviour problems, as well as math and reading score deficits, were associated with divorce or separation, even after controlling for pre-divorce scores, although reading score deficits for girls were small.

Although many studies have been completed on the effects of different family forms, a review article on divorce in the United States (Furstenberg 1990) revealed surprisingly little consensus on the underlying causes of children's deficits associated with divorce. Since the publication of that article, some progress has been made with respect to the understanding of how divorce affects children, including the roles of family structure, social processes associated with changes in family form, and the development of models of the mechanisms by which children's health, educational, and behavioural deficits are created.

Models explaining children's deficits can emphasize the role of family structure (for example, two-parent versus one-parent families) or process, that is, divorce, in the creation of these deficits. If the effects of process can be held constant, the contribution of structure to children's deficits can be more clearly examined. For example, neither never-married single parents nor always-married two-parent families have experienced divorce. Since the structure of the family has not changed, the outcomes for children in these two family forms should show the effects of one versus two parents. Studies that differentiate between single-parent homes due to divorce and those of a never-married parent find that both of these marital statuses are associated with deficits in children, even after controlling for the lower socio-economic status in never-married families (Thomson, Hanson, and McLanahan 1994). In other words, along virtually every measure, children of never-married single parents have educational, behavioural, and health deficits compared to children in intact families. Ergo, there appears to be an important effect of family structure on children's outcomes, with children significantly benefiting from two-parent families.

Similarly, if the effects of family structure are held constant, the effects of process on children can be estimated. For example, a single-parent family can occur through divorce or through the death of a parent. Studies that compare children who live in the same one-parent family structure but have experienced either divorce or the death of a parent find that the effect of divorce has more serious consequences for children's welfare than does the loss of a parent through death, even after controlling for the relatively lower levels of income among divorced single parents (Aquilino 1994). Thus, the process of divorce as opposed to the loss of a parent through death appears to play a role in the creation of deficits for children, perhaps because the deceased parent symbolically remains a source of support for the child, while divorce can often see the child adopting the hostility of one of the parents towards the other. Another case in which the effects of process can be gauged is in comparing children living in divorced and then remarried families with families that have remained intact. Again, the evidence here is that children in remarried families fare worse than children in intact, two-parent families (Kim 2002). Moreover, when comparing children in divorced single-parent families with children in families where a parent has remarried, very little benefit (some studies find none) is obtained by the addition of a step-parent, even though a large increase in household income is associated with remarriage (Cherlin and Furstenberg 1994).

The previous discussion illustrates that there appears to be important effects on children's outcomes associated with *both* family structure and the divorce process. Perhaps the most powerful of these effects is in the interaction of the two; that is, when there are two parents and they do not divorce, which appears to provide children with the greatest chances for success. Coleman (1990) explained the importance of both structure and process in creating these effects by looking at parents as a resource to children. Thus, two parents are a greater resource than one, and smaller family sizes, given the same number of parents, represent a greater resource, through improved supervision and guidance in addition to the reduced stress on the parents through work sharing and better financial resources to the children in the family. The maintenance of two parents allows a greater degree of trust between the parent and child, which enables long-term patterns of learning. Further, the presence of both parents from birth allows the development of consistent and reinforcing relations between the generations, which magnifies parent-child trust, allowing a more direct transfer of human capital. The addition of a step-parent after divorce requires many years of adjustment before the same kind of parental consistency, cooperation, and trust can be established, and, hence, is less successful at enabling children's adjustment.

Models of children's outcomes in the context of divorce employ several causal mechanisms in explaining how the deficits found in children of divorced parents occur. I have already discussed theories surrounding the direct effect of divorce through changes in family structure; other indirect causal mechanisms include the *selectivity* perspective, the intervening or *strain* model, and perspectives that argue that difficulties experienced by children of divorce are not due to divorce itself, but caused by other variables – the *spurious* perspective (Simons 1996).

The selectivity perspective asserts that the people self-selected into the process of divorce are different along important traits that affect children than are people who do not divorce. For example, people who divorce might be over-represented in terms of, say, antisocial tenden-

Figure 3.1: Selectivity Model

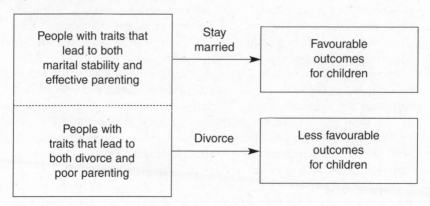

cies, which would account for differences in parenting that lead to less favourable outcomes for children (see Figure 3.1).

This model consequently asserts that it is not divorce per se that causes less favourable outcomes for children, but rather the individual differences in traits important to the parenting of children. The selectivity perspective agrees with social capital theory in that differences in parenting ability would explain degradations in children's outcomes. However, social capital theory also predicts, contrary to the selectivity perspective, that divorce will have an important additional independent negative impact on children due to the loss or degradation of relationships available to the child. The selectivity argument has not been sufficiently investigated empirically, perhaps because statistical techniques to deal with this issue have only recently been made available and are complex. However, there are some reasons to believe that selectivity does not entirely explain the effects of divorce on children.

First, the incidence of divorce is highly related to the legal barriers to the dissolution of a marriage. For example, divorce was rare in Canada before the enactment of the first federal divorce law in 1968, and increased dramatically thereafter. The second Divorce Act (1986) similarly decreased the barriers to divorce, and there was an ensuing surge in the number of people filing for divorce. Selectivity, therefore, cannot explain the large variations in the divorce rate over time when presumably the characteristics of people that would select divorce did not change in 1968 and 1986. Moreover, a study that examined the effects of divorce on educational attainment over time (Evans, Kelley, and Wanner 2001) showed that these negative effects of divorce on this measure of children's success are becoming stronger, not weaker, as divorce becomes easier. Again, it would be difficult to argue that the characteristics of parents are worsening. Also, the divorce rate is large: roughly 38 per cent of marriages in Canada are expected to fail before the 30th wedding anniversary (Statistics Canada 2004), so the number of people divorcing is likely to contain a great deal of variation in individual traits. Selectivity alone is, then, unlikely to explain a large proportion of children's deficits associated with the experience of divorce.

The spurious perspective asserts that less favourable outcomes for children of divorce are due to some external factor, such as lower income or higher inter-parental conflict, as opposed to divorce itself or some personal characteristic of divorcing parents. Thus, the divorced and nondivorced are not necessarily significantly different, as in the selectivity argument, but a common cause, such as inter-parental conflict or low income, causes both divorce and less beneficial outcomes for children. That is, divorce per se is not the cause of the deficits in children associated with divorce (see Figure 3.2). This perspective is fundamentally at odds with social capital theory because it does not allow for an independent effect for the changes in relationships associated with divorce. Coleman would, however, predict an effect from inter-parental conflict since it is deleterious to the process of cooperation, which he uses to explain the success of intact families. The empirical evidence for the association of inter-parental conflict on children supports an association with detrimental effects, even after controlling for marital status. However, I am not aware of a study that shows that it removes the effects of divorce completely. Income or social class, on the other hand, does not appear to be an important factor in any model that measures children's behavioural outcomes if measures of parenting are included as an explanatory variable. Thus, although inter-parental conflict is a potential common cause, since it appears to affect children whether their parents are married or divorced, it does not appear to explain all the effects of divorce on children.

A third mechanism is the so-called strain model (or intervening model), in which divorce causes emotional and/or financial strain on the parents, whose psychological adjustment and ability to parent is then impaired, causing the deficits in children associated with divorce. As with the preceding mechanisms, there is no effect of divorce, except through the strain that it causes. The intervening or strain model is

Figure 3.2: Spurious Model

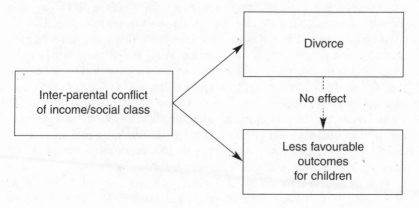

perhaps the most compatible perspective with social capital theory since it argues that variation in the ability to parent is the proximate cause of less beneficial outcomes for children. Under the strain model, divorce produces intervening economic and psychological strain in the parent(s), which consequently degrades parenting ability and hence outcomes for children (see Figure 3.3).

This research will look at children's outcomes as impacted by measures of the parental relationship, along with effects on parenting ability, as postulated by the strain model given in Figure 3.3. An article which reviewed the empirical findings of more than 100 studies of children who had experienced divorce (Amato 1993) found consistent empirical support for the following explanatory variables on children's outcomes after divorce: parental psychological adjustment, parenting behaviours, inter-parental conflict, and quality of the parent-child relationship. These variables, with the possible exception of inter-parental conflict, are all factors that would be expected to worsen under conditions of parental strain, such as is frequently experienced in the context of divorce. Thus, these results would support the contention of the strain model, as well as the direct effects of family structure and parenting on the child. That is, the effects of divorce on children are highly affected by the quality of the parent-child relationship. Few studies completely remove the effects of divorce even after controlling for the intervening effects of these factors, so the contention of Coleman that the presence of two parents with the cooperation and consistency enabled by unbroken parental bonds still appears to have

Figure 3.3: Strain (Intervening) Model

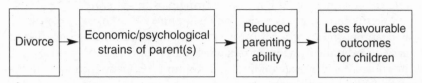

explanatory value. That is, two parents, presumably through improved supervision and guidance and through the greater availability of parental resources, provide improved outcomes for their children compared to a single parent acting alone. Both the process of divorce – directly and indirectly through strain – as well as family structure appear to have important consequences for the well-being of children.

The theories and research in the academic world of social science provide us with the foregoing analysis of the effects of divorce on children. Custody evaluations are an important component of custody determination processes. Custody evaluators have their own procedures, practices, and theoretical assumptions that do not necessarily coincide with the previously discussed research. Because of the potentially influential impact of custody evaluators on court decisions, I will deal with the paradigm and procedures involved with custody evaluation, including issues surrounding the people involved with requesting and performing these evaluations. First, however, I turn to the most influential legal theory about the best interests of the child.

The Legal Paradigm of Custody Determination: Primary Caregiver

The primary caregiver presumption is a legal presumption for custody as well as a theoretical framework for understanding child development and how the law ought to intervene in the interests of children. The development of the primary caregiver presumption has been strongly bolstered by a series of highly influential books by Goldstein, Solnit, and Freud (1973, 1979, 1986; Goldstein et al. 1996), which target the custody decision-making process and prescribe the legal parameters for custody to be considered in family jurisprudence. The following discussion will treat these books as one body of work, since the books are interrelated, available as a single volume, and a prominent part of the general theoretical structure that dominates custody law and the formulation of family law principles in general.

The first book in this series, published in 1973, and its sequels have had an enormous impact on legal thinking about child custody and access. A detailed review of this work is appropriate if only because of its enormous influence on the legal community. Aside from having the cachet of being co-authored by the daughter of Sigmund Freud, the founder of child psychoanalysis, the book is frequently cited in the legal literature. For example, a search using the Hein Online legal database turned up 819 citations of reviews[1] dating from its first publication in 1973 – in the 1973 Cornell, Columbia, DePaul, Fordham, Georgetown, George Washington, Hastings, Michigan, Southern California, Southwestern, Utah, William and Mary, and Yale Law Reviews – and have since been mentioned in virtually every influential American and Canadian law journal, including citations or reviews in 14 separate volumes of the *Canadian Journal of Family Law* alone. In addition, the book is cited in two of Canada's most influential Supreme Court precedents in the area of family law: *Gordon v. Goertz* (1996) and *Young v. Young* (1993). In *Young v. Young* the court was asked to adjudicate on the issue of whether religious instruction by the non-custodial parent could proceed in the face of opposition by the custodial parent. In the case of *Gordon v. Goertz*, the court was asked to decide whether the custodial parent could relocate from Canada to Australia, thereby severely degrading the heretofore warm, regular, and supportive relationship of the non-custodial parent with the child. In both these decisions, the court came down firmly on the side of the autonomy of the custodial parent and the importance of supporting the custodial parent's discretion in matters relating to the child's welfare. Moreover, the principle of the best interests of the child was deemed paramount, since the Constitution was either deemed inapplicable to the private considerations of custody and access, or, since the court deems itself to be acting on behalf of children, the children's constitutional rights are congruent with the best interests standard. In this way, the Constitution was rendered irrelevant to decisions of custody and access.

The argument of Goldstein, Solnit, and Freud begins with a description of the differences between the needs of children and adults (Goldstein et al. 1996). Five major differences are cited: children, and consequently their needs, change constantly; children experience time differently and are therefore more sensitive than an adult would be to the length of separation from a loved one; children see all events as relating to only themselves; they respond emotionally, rather than rationally, to events, which makes them vulnerable; and children have no psychological concept of the blood-tie. What matters to them are the day-to-day interactions, which are the basis for their attachments.

Thus, from the child's point of view, the importance lies with the psychological parent as opposed to the biological one. For Goldstein et al. (1996) the critical focus is to provide 'at least one psychological parent' in order to 'develop a healthy self-esteem' (13). The continuity of the relationship with the psychological parent is, thence, of prime importance for a child's development.

On the above basis, Goldstein et al. (1996) develop a series of important guidelines and discuss their implications for child placement. The first of these is the need to maintain the continuity of the psychological parent relationship for the child. Thus, once a placement is ruled upon, it should be considered 'as permanent as the assignment of a newborn to her biological parents' (20). With respect to access or visitation, the authors are clear: contact with the non-custodial parent is more of a risk than a benefit for children of separation or divorce since loyalty conflicts may destroy the positive aspects of the child's relationship with both parents. Thus, the authors recommend no legally enforceable right for the non-custodial parent to visit the child, except where the custodial parent is favourably disposed to such visits. Further, this recommendation is extended to grandparents. Nonetheless, the authors recommend that separating parents be allowed to make any custody or access arrangement that they desire, and make it clear that visits are not necessarily harmful: it is just that they must be at the discretion of the custodial parent. As a corollary to this assertion, the authors recommend that the child be placed with the parent most likely to facilitate visits. This assertion seems somewhat paradoxical, given the emphasis the authors have placed on the paramountcy of the autonomy of the custodial parent, and hence the relative unimportance of the relation with the non-custodial parent.

Further to the support of autonomy of the custodial parent, Goldstein et al. (1996) discourage joint or split custody arrangements since they regard these arrangements as tantamount to forced visitation. The authors cite a variety of legal precedents, including one by Justice Abella (33), now on Canada's Supreme Court, emphasizing the concurrence of the judiciary on the importance of supporting the wishes of the custodial over the non-custodial parent in judicial decisions regarding custody and access. Therefore, in the view of these authors, the 'best interests' test is best served by selecting one parent over the other and strongly supporting the custodial parent's unfettered autonomy and control over the child, and that parent's decisions about the welfare of the child. The court's concern about the relationship and access of the non-custodial parent to the child is characterized as treating the child like a material good to be distributed among the divorcing parents. This view of the importance of the custodial parent versus the non-custodial parent is constructed as proceeding from the rights of the child, not of the custodial parent. Thus, since it is in the child's best interest not to see the non-custodial parent, except as is consistent with the preferences of the custodial parent, the right of the child to avoid contact with the non-custodial parent must be respected (38). It follows as a matter of course that the custodial parent be able to move without restriction, regardless of how it might impact on the relationship with the non-custodial parent. Mobility rights of either parent, according to these authors, do not cross the threshold of consideration since the best interests of the child, while not constitutionally entrenched, are of primary concern.

In order to respect the child's sense of time, the court is encouraged to place the child as a matter of urgency. Hence, custody hearings must be conducted with all possible haste, preferably preceding other determinations, such as support, access, and property division.

According to these authors, the job of the courts is not to decide what is in the best interests of the child. This is presented as a task beyond the capacity of the courts to determine. Rather, the courts are charged with a task that is, at least according to the authors, well within their grasp: to choose *who* is in the best interests of the child, from among the available candidates (usually, but not limited to, the mother and the father), and, once that decision is made, to endow that individual with virtually unfettered capacity to raise the child as he or she sees fit. The selection of the best parent should be guided by the principle of the least detrimental alternative. That is, the custodial parent should be chosen on the lack of capacity to harm the child, as opposed to, say, the greatest capacity to benefit the child, in a model analogous to the medical maxim, 'First, do no harm.'

Goldstein et al. (1996) deal with exceptions to their general assertion that the courts must avoid intrusion into the lives of children, since in their minds such state intrusion is an unwelcome and unhealthy imposition on the development of children. Thus, they outline seven specific situations which nevertheless call for such intrusion: when the parents ask the court to determine placement of the child's custody; when the parents no longer wish to care for the child; when natural parents wish to regain custody from long-term caregivers; when parents have died or disappeared without leaving instructions for the care of their child(ren); when parents seriously harm their children; when parents refuse to provide lifesaving medical care; and when the child requires separate and independent legal counsel.

In *The Best Interests of the Child* (1996) the authors emphasize the need for judicial discipline in remaining within the limits of their expertise. However, they are ambivalent, concurrently arguing that judges must not be overly obedient to the recommendations of experts.

The authors compare three often-used standards for child custody determination: gender (preference for the mother, also known as the 'Tender Years Doctrine'), blood-tie (preference for biological ties over social ones), and the primary caregiver presumption. The authors strongly endorse the primary caregiver presumption because it most closely follows the ideas they have previously presented regarding the prime importance of at least one psychological parent in the child's life (193). The indications of the primary caregiver are many, but, as listed by the authors, are largely related to activities incidental to child care, such as meal preparation, bathing and grooming the child, purchasing food and other goods related to the child's needs, and transporting the child to activities. Also listed are activities such as educating, teaching, and disciplining, although specific behaviours are not noted (191). The authors assert that these criteria are not definitive and ought to be open to review, challenge, and change. These indicia of the primary caregiver – and therefore the all-important role of psychological parent – although at one time unambiguously performed by mothers, are in more recent times performed by either parent, or, increasingly, by third parties such as day-care workers. Nonetheless, the main contention of Goldstein, Solnit, and Freud, that a single psychological parent satisfies a child's need after divorce, has been extremely influential in legal forums, to the point that the non-custodial parent's potential contribution to child-rearing is considered unimportant, aside from any financial contributions that he or she may make. For example, an important precedent from Alberta's highest court asserts that when determining child support, considerations of the non-custodial parent's welfare are irrelevant, unless the non-custodial parent has been reduced to abject poverty, obviously discounting any non-financial contribution a non-custodial parent might make to the raising of his or her children (Levesque v. Levesque 1994: 329). Thus, the legal effect of Goldstein, Solnit, and Freud's arguments has been to regard the non-custodial parent as beneficial to the child only as a financial resource.

Criticisms of Goldstein, Solnit, and Freud

Since the arguments of Goldstein, Solnit, and Freud are widely accepted in the legal community, it is important to consider criticisms of the authors and the primary caregiver presumption to ensure that the dominant framework of family law remains true to social science findings since the original publication of their work. At least two other efforts have been made to criticize the position taken by these books. In 'Who Owns the Child? Divorce and Child Custody Decisions in Middle-Class Families,' Stack (1976) argues that the prescription of leaving the decision of visitation in the hands of the custodial parent is not in the best interests of the child, although the argument is based on theoretical and logical considerations since little empirical evidence was available at the time of writing. In a review article on the first book of the series, Katkin, Bullington, and Levine (1974) criticize the book for lack of evidence to support its claims, and cast doubt on the workability of its proposals. Again, little empirical evidence was available at the time of writing to bolster their concerns.

I intend to criticize the approach offered by Goldstein, Solnit, and Freud by marshalling a growing body of social science research to show how empirical evidence throws the main assertions of this influential work into question. These criticisms can be grouped into two main areas. First, the contention of the supremacy of the psychological parent, and the derivative conclusions resulting from it, conflict with empirical evidence of such a policy on children's outcomes. Similarly, the conclusions drawn by the authors with respect to joint custody and visitation, as well as the radical discounting of the biological aspect of the parent-child relation, face growing contrary evidence. Second, the criteria listed for the – to the authors – all-important choice of custodial parent is not based on criteria that evidence associates with the best available parent.

The criteria presented by the Goldstein, Solnit, and Freud in the 'Best Interests' series are based on a few clearly delineated principles. First, a child needs 'at least one' psychological parent, and the continuity of that relationship (and only that relationship) is paramount.

Further, due to the importance of this single relation and the need to avoid the ancillary effects of interference with the autonomy of that one parent, the courts should provide an environment where any restriction of that autonomy is legally prevented. Thus, access or visitation by the non-custodial parent should proceed only at the discretion of the custodial parent. The assumption made by the authors is that the distress caused by any interference in the custodial parent's autonomy will be visited upon the child in the form of loyalty conflicts. This framework, while providing easy to follow guidelines for the court, is not supported by empirical social science evidence. For example, the benefit to children of the two-parent intact family is one of the most consistent findings in sociology of the family research. Few studies find that children within single-parent families are accorded the same life chances as they are in families with both parents, be they never-married or divorced, and most support the opposite conclusion (Amato and Sobolewski 2001; Cherlin et al. 1991; Ely et al. 1999; Furstenberg, Hoffman, and Shrestha 1995; Mauldon 1990). Moreover, the blood-tie that the authors suggest is unimportant also appears to have important beneficial effects for children. Children fare better in two-parent biological families than in two-parent stepfamilies (Cherlin and Furstenberg 1994), another well-established finding in the sociology of the family. Moreover, children are far more likely to be abused by non-biological parents than by biological ones: Daly and Wilson (1988) assert that it is the 'single most powerful risk factor for child abuse that has yet been identified' (87–8). Recent research suggests that this is true of stepmothers as well as stepfathers (Harris et al. 2005). Thus, the major tenet of Goldstein, Solnit, and Freud's thesis – one that has been adopted wholeheartedly by many jurists, including the Supreme Court of Canada – is not only unsupported by evidence, but, worse, appears to promote harmful outcomes for children through the legal support given the destruction of one of the important parental relationships for the child.

One contention made by Goldstein, Solnit, and Freud regarding the importance of the continuation of important relationships for children, *is* supported by the preponderance of social science evidence. However, the main source for this evidence is the literature on divorce, which suggests that the destruction or denigration of a major supportive relation for the child – the non-custodial parent – is associated with a wide range of deficits for children. The approach of Goldstein, Solnit, and Freud – that the destruction of one relationship is not harmful, as long as one of the parental relations is maintained – seems difficult to defend.

The argument that interference with the autonomy of the custodial parent, at least when it is interference by the other biological parent, also seems to be problematic. While married, the autonomy of each parent with respect to parenting decisions is – typically – constantly interfered with and moderated by the other parent. Yet it is this arrangement, not the one proposed by the authors, that provides benefits for children. Increased supervision, not only of the children but of the parents by each other, seems to correlate with better results in terms of measurable outcomes for children. Loyalty conflicts may indeed arise more often post- than pre-divorce. However, the literature does not support the detrimental effects foreseen by Goldstein, Solnit, and Freud. While definitive studies concerning the effects of access or visitation on children are few, there is little evidence to support the authors' contention that this is harmful unless it is at the discretion of the custodial parent. Indeed, the unfettered autonomy of one parent may have harmful consequences for children.

Joint custody in particular appears to have beneficial effects for children. For example, a study of the effect of joint custody on children's adjustment found that fewer child adjustment problems were associated with joint custody, controlling for pre-divorce selection factors and inter-parental conflict (Gunnoe and Braver 2001). A meta-analysis of 33 studies dating from 1982 to 1999 – 11 published, 21 doctoral dissertations, and one other unpublished study – comparing child adjustment in joint and sole custody settings found that children in joint custody settings were better adjusted along a wide range of measures, even after controlling for inter-parental conflict (Bauserman 2002). Seltzer (1998) likewise found that joint custody had a positive impact on father-child visitation. In contrast, Donnelly and Finkelhorn (1992) found no significant difference between the amount of parent-child support and parent-child disagreements by custody type, and that sole custodial parents reported higher support from their children. On the other hand, interviews of young adults whose parents divorced suggest that children's adjustment was positively correlated to equal time arrangements with both parents (Fabricius 2003).

I now turn to the criteria suggested by Goldstein, Solnit, and Freud (1996) for determining the primary psychological parent. Although these indications were not developed by the authors (they come from an American legal precedent; Garska v. McCoy 1981), they are nonetheless reified by them, though they supply the caveat that they are 'open to change, challenge and debate' (191). I reproduce them here:

(1) preparing and planning of meals;
(2) bathing, grooming, and dressing;
(3) purchasing, cleaning, and care of clothes;
(4) medical care, including nursing and trips to physicians;
(5) arranging for social interaction among peers after school; i.e., transporting to friends' houses or, for example, to boy or girl scout meetings;
(6) arranging alternative care, i.e., babysitting, daycare, etc.;
(7) putting child to bed at night, attending to child in the middle of the night; waking child in the morning;
(8) disciplining, i.e., teaching general manners and toilet training;
(9) educating, i.e., religious, cultural, social, etc.; and
(10) teaching elementary skills, i.e., reading, writing, and arithmetic.

Although these indications, which could be summarized as housework and childcare, were evidently designed to correspond to activities at one time traditionally performed by women (no traditionally male parenting and home care activities are specifically mentioned – coaching sports, maintenance of home and vehicle, playing with the child, and yard work, for example), changing gender roles have already produced a near equal performance of childcare by gender, according to a recent study by Health Canada (Higgins and Duxbury 2002). Moreover, most of the activities mentioned are related to the care of younger children (children of 'tender years').

The indicia listed above could easily identify a day-care worker as the primary caretaker over a parent. Moreover, according to the authors, these indicators are neither constant nor uncontested, rendering the concepts of 'psychological parent' and 'primary caregiver' somewhat vague, with indicators that are various and broad enough to allow the support or contradiction of virtually any custody assignment that does not involve obvious evidence of potential future harm to the child. Further, the indicators are generally behavioural, but no indications are given as to the relative importance of the behaviours, nor how the length of time engaged in any particular behaviour might relate to the determination of primary or psychological parent. No psychological traits or conditions, nor specific parenting behaviours, appear to be marshalled as potential indicators of the primary care-taker. Moreover, little research supports the use of these activities as an indication of superiority in the parental role, at least as measured by beneficial outcomes for children.

The ability to discern parental traits and behaviours with known correlation to children's behavioural health and educational outcomes would seem to present an alternative to the primary caretaker approach, whose effects on children are less well-known. Given the deficits in children associated with divorce, there may be room for improvement in the system as it currently operates.

Before I turn to the other research on the assessment of children's interest, I will first attend to the framework and dynamics of professional child custody evaluators.

Custody Evaluations

The ideas and research results of the social science, and especially sociology, academy, while related, reside in a different context than custody evaluations. The ultimate question of custody determination is in the hands of a judge if the matter goes to trial. The custody determination is therefore strongly influenced by legal norms and ideas about custody in the legal field. Like the sociological ideas discussed in the previous section, legal ideas about parenting and children, the subject of a later section in this work, do not necessarily coincide with the ideas from the field of psychology, which can become influential if a custody evaluation is undertaken as part of the divorce process. It is to this process of custody evaluation by external experts that we now turn to examine what precipitates a custody evaluation, what it entails, and what factors custody evaluators use to determine who is the parent most suited for the custody of the child or children.

This section explores questions related to the role of custody evaluators in the custody assignment process. For example, it asks why judges and lawyers make use of the services of third-party evaluators and what criteria evaluators use to determine custody arrangement recommendations. Moreover, the methods that evaluators use to gather the information upon which to base their recommendations are examined, as well as emerging custody evaluation systems marketed by prominent custody evaluation experts.

Judges do not usually order a custody evaluation in the course of a divorce hearing or trial, since it is not their role to determine which evidence should be presented to the court.[2] Thus, it is up to one or the other of the parties involved to request a custody evaluation. Nevertheless, judges usually look favourably on the involvement of a custody evaluator since they feel that in the reports generated by the process, although designed for the consumption of the judge, the child's interests will be given foremost consideration (Houghton 1995). Moreover, engaging a custody evaluator is an opportunity to delegate a decision that, while central to many divorce cases, is not usually something that judges are trained to do. The only qualification for becoming a judge in Canada is experience as a lawyer. Most judges, then, have a law degree, and although they frequently possess a degree in another discipline, are provided with little training in the interviewing of children. Indeed, the interview training afforded lawyers is pertinent to the litigation process, which entails interviewing with an eye to eliciting information or an end result that the questioner desires, which would seem to be an orientation detrimental to the process required for interviewing a witness whose reality is as fragile and as easily influenced as a child's. Moreover, child witnesses appear to be problematic in a number of respects: while children can usually distinguish the difference between lying and telling the truth, this has little bearing on whether they are truthful (Bala et al. 2000; Talwar et al. 2002). Moreover, most people – including judges – are unable to distinguish whether a child is telling the truth or lying, and overestimate the truthfulness of children as well (Bala et al. 2005; Talwar et al. 2004). Thus, the child custody evaluator is a welcome delegation of authority for the thorny issue of custody determination for many judges.

Lawyers, on the other hand, are seen as having a variety of objectives that interact with the possibility of a child custody evaluation. MacNaughton (1995) categorizes lawyers according to these motives as advocates, problem solvers, and client managers. These categories are not necessarily mutually exclusive, but are intended to shed some light on some of the intentions that a given legal counsel may have in a divorce case. *Advocates* are lawyers who see themselves as acting on their client's behalf in such a fashion as to achieve victory in the context of the adversarial process. They are, therefore, only likely to recommend a custody evaluation if they perceive it to enhance their client's chances of winning in court. *Problem solvers*, on the other hand, are lawyers who see the custody determination as a problem to be solved, and the custody evaluation provides a means of obtaining additional useful information and a means of conflict reduction in a potentially less contentious way than through the legal process. *Client managers* are lawyers who are seeking ways in which to better control their client. The evaluation may be ordered by such a lawyer in order to better understand their client and as a way of managing their client's expectations with respect to a possible hearing in court. Hence, lawyers may have a variety of reasons for seeking a child custody evaluation.

In addition to the motivations of attorneys, there are other forces which come to bear on the possibility of a child custody evaluation, the chief of which is whether it can be paid for, either by the clients, or, in the rare case where the court deems it appropriate, by the state. Plainly, child custody evaluations are more likely to occur among wealthier clients and high-conflict clients, who can bear the cost of a child custody evaluator along with the attendant legal fees that are involved in a case where there is enough disagreement to require a custody evaluation. A survey of judges in the Midwestern United States identified 'excessive costs' and 'lack of resources of clients' as the biggest obstacle to the performance of a child custody evaluation (Waller and Daniel 2004). Roughly 20 years ago, Keilin and Bloom (1986) estimated that the average cost of an evaluation was U.S. $965 among 82 child custody evaluators, who were mainly psychologists. Bricklin suggests the average cost in American urban areas is roughly U.S. $2,000 for a typical custody evaluation, although costs in exceptional cases exceeded U.S. $7,000 (1995:223). Ackerman and Ackerman (1997) report that 'the average cost of a custody evaluation was $2,646. The range of average fees for custody evaluations was $650 to $15,000. The average fee for a custody evaluation has almost tripled in the past 10 years.' Custody evaluation is becoming an increasingly expensive proposition for divorcing couples, who are likely already experiencing large outlays in the form of legal fees. It follows from the previous discussion that the performance of custody evaluations, like the decision to contest custody in court, is contingent upon a number of factors not necessarily relating to the parent involved, including the disposition of the lawyer as well as costs. I do not intend to use this dynamic to explain court decisions; rather, it should be apparent that contingencies involved in a legal dispute are not necessarily centred on anything resembling a concern for the best interests of the child.

Who Performs Custody Evaluations?

Custody evaluators appear to derive mainly from two professional disciplines: psychology and social work, although a variety of other qualifications may be involved. For example, a guideline on custody evaluations published by the Association of Family and Conciliation Courts (AFCC) contains articles written by PhD psychologists, social workers with a Master of Social Work degree (MSW), and one PhD of social work, but also includes a variety of other qualifications such as a Master of Science degree, a 'Marriage, Family and Child Counsellor,' and a 'Licensed Clinical Social Worker' (Bushard and Howard 1995). However, most books describing how to perform custody evaluations, and targeted at custody evaluators, are written by PhD psychologists (Ackerman 2001; Bricklin 1995; Gould 1998; Skafte 1985; Stahl 1999) and psychiatrists (Marafiote 1985). Custody evaluations may therefore be performed by people with a variety of backgrounds and qualifications, the foremost of which are psychologists and social workers; however, the most influential appear to be psychologists with doctoral-level training.

How Do Custody Evaluators Gather Information?

Custody evaluators invariably recommend gathering ·information about the family members involved in a custody evaluation, but the recommended methods of obtaining this information, along with the kind of information sought, varies. Methods of information gathering include observation of children in clinical or other settings; observation of parent and child together in clinical or other contexts; interviews of parents, either together or separately; psychological assessments of parents and children; interviewing relatives, friends, new spouses, or other individuals; as well as interviewing or obtaining materials such as reports from third parties such as educators, health professionals, childcare and social workers, or agencies that may have had involvement with any of the parties. While most guidelines suggest use of multiple methods of information gathering (Ackerman 2001; American Psychological Association 1994; Skafte 1985; Stahl 1999), there appears to be no hard and fast list of specific procedures that must be included in a custody evaluation for it to be complete. According to a recent study of custody evaluation practices, the top-ranked procedures among psychologists were: clinical interviews with parents, clinical interviews with the children, parent-child observations, psychological testing of the parents, history of the child(ren) according to the parents, and psychological testing of the child(ren) (Quinnell and Bow 2001).

The use of psychological tests are commonly conducted in the course of child custody evaluations performed by psychologists, and this use has been growing (Ackerman and Ackerman 1997; Quinnell and Bow 2001). Although the use of psychological testing by other professionals is not well documented, it would seem logical to assume that their use is reduced when the administration of such a test is beyond the training of the professional involved, that is, when the evaluator is not a psychologist. The most-often-used instrument for adults appears to be the original or second-edition version of the Minnesota Multiphasic Personality Inventory (MMPI), an objective personality test which was used by 94 per cent of the 198 American custody evaluators in Quinnell and Bow's study (2001). A second objective personality test, the Millon Clinical Multiaxial Inventory (MCMI-III), appears to be gaining popularity. Adults are also – less frequently – assessed with projective personality instruments, such as the Rorschach ink blot test and the Sentence Completion test. The use of intelligence and academic competency tests for children, while still common, appears to be declining. While projective tests were the main instruments used for children, there appears to be a reduction in the interest in testing of children in favour of testing parents for psychopathologies, as well as for items thought to correlate with parenting ability (ibid.). The argument for using psychological tests includes contentions that certain psychopathologies, such as depression, can be diagnosed using these tests and are associated with negative outcomes for children, and that mental health professionals and indeed judges and lawyers cannot reliably detect lies. Thus, relying on interviews alone is less reliable than combining them with psychological tests (Nims 1995).

Judges and lawyers expect interviews of all the protagonists in the custody decision as part of custody evaluations (Ackerman 2001:93). Directions for interviewing parents typically review family history and assess the appropriateness of parents' plans by exercises such as having the parent imagine potential scenarios following divorce: how arrangements might play out if that parent had custody, and how the parent would deal with the possibility of not winning custody (Skafte

1985). Others emphasize the importance of assessing the parental emotional adjustment to the divorce; for example, Bushard (1995) recommends interviewing parents to determine the emphasis each parent places on the future versus the past, and whether he or she is focused on the behaviour of themselves or that of others.

Interviewing children presents special difficulties, since directly questioning children on their preference for custody arrangements may result in undue stress on the child (Hodges 1991:131; Stahl 1999:71), although, like Bricklin (1995:237), I could find no research on this specific subject. In any event, most psychologists do not accept the wishes of the child to be determinative until the age of 15 (Ackerman and Ackerman 1997). The issue of custody is explored gingerly with a variety of indirect techniques and measures. For example, to assess the degree of trust the child has with a parent, the interviewer might ask the child to imagine various scenarios where he or she needed help, and ask who the child would go to for assistance (Skafte 1985:109). Children are also asked to draw their family, with the proximity of each parent in the drawing serving as a proxy for the emotional closeness the child has with that parent. This exercise can be performed with one or both parents and in different contexts (Bricklin 1995:813). One reference, part of the Association of Family and Conciliation Courts' recommended practices, offers many strategies for conducting interviews with children. Some of these strategies are targeted at understanding the child's developmental issues, feelings towards each parent, and feelings towards the events in his or her life that are related to the divorce; others, however, are targeted at using the child as an informant to understand and assess parents and parental interaction. For example, one guideline suggests asking the child about parental behaviour, such as, 'Show me what happens when Dad comes to pick you up and you leave Mom,' and 'Let's pretend Dad calls you. What does he say to you?' (Vasquez 1995). Thus, while most approaches to interviewing children use indirect techniques to assess the emotional quality of the relation of the child to each parent, some use the child as a reporter on more general issues related to the behaviour of the parents. This latter approach, given the lack of reliability of child witnesses, as discussed above, may be problematic, even if one is comfortable with the moral issues involved with using the child as an informant on parents. While the previous examples show the stress some researchers place on using children as a means of gaining information about parents, other researchers feel that the most salient path to useful knowledge about the parent-child relationship is through the child's perception of the relationship expressed non-verbally (Bricklin 1995:74).

From the preceding discussion it can be seen that although the steps involved in a custody evaluation, such as interviewing children, may be present in virtually all such assessments, the procedures used and the emphasis placed upon them vary considerably.

What Factors Do Child Custody Evaluators Use to Determine Custody?

A recent study of psychologists who perform custody evaluations listed the following as the five most influential factors for a parent to lose custody (that is, for sole custody to be assigned to the other parent):

1. Parent is an alcoholic
2. Parent tries to alienate the child from the other parent
3. The other parent exhibits better parenting
4. Child has a stronger emotional bond with the other parent
5. Parent is less psychologically stable than the other parent

The least influential factors, on the other hand, involve the post-divorce family structure and issues of the age and gender of the children and parents (Ackerman and Ackerman 1997). The same study lists issues related to inter-parental conflict as important when considering joint custody. These factors are consistent with a review of the empirical evidence related to children's adjustment after divorce, since parental alienation can be conceptualized as destroying the emotional bond of the child with the other parent, although there appears to be little research on the effects of parental alienation on children. The emotional bond of the child with the parent is universally considered an important aspect of a custody decision, and enjoys at least some empirical support (Amato 1993; Amato and Gilbreth 1999). It is interesting to note that although the meaning of the custody criteria listed above may, on the surface, seem plain, there is no agreed-upon measurement of some of these concepts. For example, while the fourth edition of the *Diagnostic and Statistical Manual of Mental Disorders* has definitions for substance dependence and substance abuse, there is no definition for parental alienation of a child, despite the efforts of

Gardner (1987, 1998), who coined the term 'Parental Alienation Syndrome' (PAS). There is no recognized measure of this concept, nor of its more general cousin, 'Malicious Parent Syndrome'(Turkat 1999), at least not one that has been empirically verified and accepted by the psychological community. Nonetheless, most custody evaluation books mention the phenomenon of parental alienation as something that evaluators must be cognizant of (Ackerman 2001; Gould 1998; Stahl 1999).

With respect to parenting behaviours, there are some measures available (Strayhorn and Weidman, 1988); however, the relative importance of each of the behaviours and their effect on child outcomes is not well researched. Similarly, while there are theoretical connections with various psychopathological measures from the MMPI and the ability to parent and subsequent child outcomes (Ackerman 2001:132–41; Nims 1995), the empirical aspect of these connections have not been well explored. Hence, although certain scales within the MMPI, when elevated, may be indications for custody of one parent or the other, the relative importance of each measure and the likely effect and its magnitude on children's outcomes is unknown. A replication of the Ackerman and Ackerman (1997) study among psychologists in Virginia whom attorneys rated as 'credible' agreed on the first three items, but substituted 'the other parent is more tolerant of visitation' and 'before the divorce the other parent had primary caretaking responsibilities' as the fourth and fifth most important criteria (Gourley and Stolberg 2000). It is not clear whether the difference on the last two items is due to differences between American and Virginian psychologists or whether the criteria relating to the 'friendly parent' rule and 'primary caretaker' presumptions both, as we shall see, important in the legal domain influence the degree to which attorneys see psychologists as credible. A major conclusion of this study was that there was little standardization in the training of evaluators or in the methods of custody evaluation, and thus it is difficult to assess the adequacy of a given evaluation (21).

The preceding discussion of custody decision criterion gives an overly orderly account of a discipline that is far from settled or consensual as to the importance or ranking of factors to be considered when deciding custody. Each book on the subject provides a different account of both procedural and substantive issues of importance in the evaluation, and it is far from clear, even within a given work, precisely how the custody decision is arrived at. Further, some of the procedures recommended, such as using the children to inform on their parents, may be ethically questionable. Hence, even though many questions remain unsettled with respect to the relative importance of factors in custody decisions that will be most representative of a child's best interests, the field is even more contested and disorderly than the survey of psychologists presented by Ackerman and Ackerman would suggest. Moreover, the wide range of data collection and the wide discretion in its interpretation would seem to allow significant variation in the results of the evaluation depending on the evaluator and the specific instance. That is, it is unclear whether custody evaluations would end up with the same result if repeated or performed by a different evaluator or different instrument. I am not aware of any study that has attempted to gauge this issue of reliability, making this an important subject for further study in the area of custody evaluation.

Custody Evaluation Systems

In recent years, custody evaluation experts have developed products that are attempts at providing a standardized custody evaluation procedure, complete with relevant psychological tests, checklists, interview schedules, and other procedural and substantive requirements of a custody evaluation. The outcome of these systems is a scale intended to indicate fitness for custody. The two foremost of these systems are the Ackerman-Schoendorf Parent Evaluation for Custody Test (ASPECT), the most frequently used assessment system for adults; and the Bricklin set of measures, the most frequently used assessment system for children (Ackerman and Ackerman 1997). There are other systems, such as the Custody Quotient (Gordon and Peek 1988) and the Toronto Parenting Capacity Assessment Project (Steinhauer 1993). However, these systems do not appear to be as popular, nor as systematic, as the ASPECT and Bricklin systems.

The ASPECT system (Ackerman and Schoendorf 1992) is composed of three main instruments: the observational scale, which measures the self-presentation of the parent; the social scale, which is geared to measuring the parents' inter-personal skills including parenting; and the cognitive-emotional scale, a measure 'of the cognitive and affective capacities for parenting' (Ackerman 2001:145). The first two scales are overt or behavioural, while the third scale is covert or geared towards psychological traits. These three scales combine to form the Parent Custody Index (PCI), intended to indicate the fitness of the parent for custody. An admirable feature of the ASPECT is the attempts that have been made to assess its reliability and validity. For example, when the PCI indicated a significant difference favouring one parent, that parent was awarded custody by the judge in 28 of 30 cases (161). Moreover, an unpublished study of cases where the ASPECT had been administered found that most children were more satisfied with the parent indicated by ASPECT (162). Ackerman also reports high internal and inter-rater reliability. Of course, a tool that simply replicates the existing results does not necessarily constitute an improvement or even indicate the accuracy of the instrument. On the other hand, such attempts at assessing reliability are at least an improvement over the alternative, that is, no attempt to deal with the issue of reliability. Unfortunately, this is the situation with most custody evaluation methods.

The Bricklin set of instruments is aimed at choosing the Primary Care Parent (PCP) and includes the Bricklin Perceptual Scales (BPS), the Parent Awareness Skills Survey (PASS), the Parent Perception of Child Profile (PPCP), and the Perceptions of Relationships Test (PORT) (Bricklin 1995). The BPS and PORT are aimed at assessing children 'based on the child's non-verbal perceptions rather than parental behaviour' (74). The BPS is composed of 64 questions asked to the child, 32 for each parent, to which the child responds by indicating, with a stylus, his or her answer on a scale. The PORT is a projective drawing test where the child draws 11 pictures involving family members in various groupings, which are then assessed by the evaluator. The PASS is a set of 18 childcare problems, which are given to each parent to solve. The PPCP is an attempt to measure a parent's interest in a child and assesses the parent's knowledge in eight categories: Interpersonal Relations, Daily Routine, Health History, Developmental History, School History, Fears, Personal Hygiene, and Communication Style. The PPCP is intended to be an assessment of the knowledge of the day-to-day details of a child's life, with the assumption that this knowledge best represents the parent's interest in the child and that this interest translates into improved outcomes for the child (Bricklin 1995). Bricklin claims that PORT and BPS have a high degree of agreement in their results, but suggests that the task of testing the reliability and validity of his scales may be difficult since 'There is no agreement, even conceptually, as to what constitutes a 'best' custodial arrangement ...' (194). The Bricklin tests are a welcome standardization of certain techniques; however, the approach of using the child to assess the parent-child relation needs further study to determine the accuracy of the method. It is not known, for example, if knowing more details about a child's quotidian life increases a child's life chances, or even if abusive parents know less about the details of their children's lives than do non-abusive parents. Moreover, there is little evidence which demonstrates that the particular 18 problems in the PASS and the 'interest' measured by the PPCP are predictors of beneficial outcomes for children.

While both the ASPECT and Bricklin custody evaluation systems appear to have their challenges, the approach of using a definite series of criteria holds genuine potential for scientific advancement in the field. These systems present an enormous improvement over the overly broad and subjective approaches that precede them. Nevertheless, custody evaluation appears to be a fertile area for further exploration if the criteria for assigning custody are to be associated with measurable improvements in child outcomes. As can be discerned from the previous discussion, the 'best interests of the child' standard, while universally endorsed in both legal and social science disciplines, has yet to be empirically linked to many of the criteria used in child custody evaluations. Indeed, the criteria themselves, with the exception of the custody evaluation systems reviewed here, are not defined specifically enough even to tell what the criteria are. These custody evaluation systems are, in this respect, an important step in the process of defining custody evaluations that eventually will link directly to measurable benefits for children of divorce.

The assumptions used when performing a custody evaluation are highly variable and depend on the individual evaluator, his or her professional background, and the authorities relied upon for the evaluation technique. Recently developed evaluation systems represent a promising step in terms of the reliability of custody evaluations; however, links between the criteria used in these evaluations and the adjustment of children following the custody assignment remain to be explored. Even the methods used to assess parent-child relationships appear to be contested, with some approaches measuring characteristics of the parents and their perceptions of the parent-child relation while others focus mainly on the child's perception of the relation. All of this makes custody evaluation a fertile area for further research. As O'Donohue and Bradley (1999:320) lament:

> A survey of the literature on custody evaluations makes clear the need for empirical research. There is no useful operational definition of what the

best interests of the child actually are. There is inconsistency across states of legal criteria for assessing the best interest of the child. There is a lack of consensus within the field of psychology as to what the relevant variables should be. Furthermore, there is no clear standard or guideline to direct practitioners on what instruments or measures to use to collect the 'relevant' data. The validity and reliability of standardized tests for use in custody assessments are largely unknown. Many of the assessment tools advocated by authors have no clearly established psychometric properties. Observational methods and structured interviews also have questionable validity and reliability.

The custody evaluator and his or her methods and theoretical framework are only a part of the overall picture, since the paradigms referenced by the legal community – primary caregiver in particular – are likely even more important in overall custody trends. However, it is to the least influential, but perhaps most important, area of research that I now turn: social science research on children.

Children and Resiliency

Previous studies have found that children's traits tend to be stable over time, that is, children are resilient. The idea of being resilient is normally thought of in a positive light; however, if the ingrained trait is negative, this is also stable over time. For example, in a comprehensive study of the behavioural trait of aggression Olweus (1979) reviewed 24 longitudinal studies of aggressive behaviour, as rated by clinicians, teachers, or peers, and found that successive measures of the same trait were highly correlated. To give an idea of the degree of such correlations, measures taken after one year had a zero-order Pearson correlation of roughly 0.9,[3] indicating they were very strongly correlated. The degree of correlation decreased over time, yet the measures of a given trait in a child remained correlated even after decades. Similarly, early work on the stability of IQ also suggests retest scores are correlated (Thorndike 1933), a finding confirmed by more recent studies (Mortensen et al. 2003; Slate and Jones 1997; Spangler and Sabatino 1995). Because this analysis is targeted at understanding what factors in the child's environment affect the child, net of the child's previously developed tendencies, any model that hopes to truly find the effects of aspects of the child's environment should explicitly control for the previous measurement of each outcome. That is, the effects of parenting and family should be net of the measurement taken two years previous. This analysis explicitly controls for the previously measured values for all of the children's outcomes that comprise the dependent variables in this analysis, since previous research indicates that traits in children are moderately to highly correlated from one measure to the next.

This section reviewed some of the issues related to the best interests of children in terms of issues currently considered by the law, custody evaluators, and social theory. The next chapter posits a theoretical model, based on these ideas, that is subjected to an empirical test using a nationally representative sample of children collected by Statistics Canada. This model is designed to test how the relationships between children affect their future behaviour, health, and education.

4 An Empirical Assessment of the Determinants of Children's Outcomes

Thus far I have reviewed the theoretical perspectives pertaining to the predictors of children's outcomes, and outlined the development of certain measures that were an important precursor to the ability to conduct an empirical test of the theoretical model proposed above. I now turn to a review of the theoretical model, data, and methods involved in the conducting of this empirical test.

Theoretical Model

The analysis undertaken here will employ a model designed to answer questions about the causal mechanisms related to the production of children's outcomes through parenting practices, as well as the role of parental, family, and child characteristics in this process (see Figure 4.1). The model examines the direct effect of parenting practices on children's outcomes, controlling for child, family, and parental characteristics. In a similar vein to the previously discussed models of the causal mechanisms by which divorce affects children, this model looks at the causal arguments related to the effects of parenting practices on children's outcomes. It accommodates the strain model by examining the effect of parental and family attributes on parental practices, while accommodating the selectivity argument by categorizing the parents prior to children's outcomes to see if a pre-existing parental category is important after controlling for more proximate parental behaviour. If the effects of parenting practices on children's outcomes are spurious, the model should produce no effect for parenting practices on children's outcomes after controlling for the other variables in the model. Another important question dealt with by this research is the

Figure 4.1: Theoretical Model

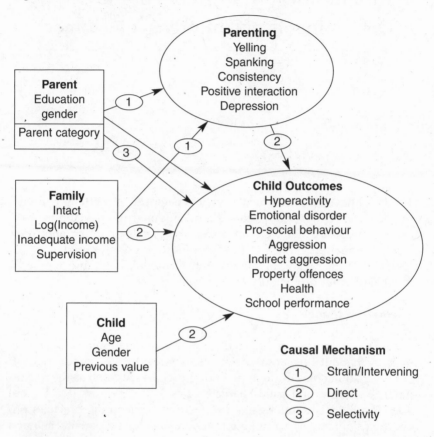

effect of a parent's gender on child outcomes. Since, as previously discussed, gender plays an important role in the production of custody determinations in Canada, a question of interest is the relationship of parent's gender to children's outcomes.

If parental gender plays an important role in the production of these outcomes, then it would follow that the apparent use of gender in custody determinations is justified. If, on the other hand, as psychologists suggest, parental gender plays only a minor role in the production of children's outcomes, it would tend to discredit the current alignment of child custody determinations along gender lines. Further, given the current lack of knowledge and consistent procedure relating to the ability to assess custody, the model can assist in providing evidence upon which to base child custody determinations in the future.

Expected Effects (Hypotheses)

The foregoing discussion of theoretical considerations leads to some expectations with respect to the effects of the explanatory variables on children's outcomes. For example, the research on children's resiliency would suggest that subsequent measures of children's characteristics would be predicted by previous measures of the same attribute. With respect to other characteristics of the child, the increased socialization experienced concurrently as a child ages would lead us to expect that children's behaviour will improve as they age, while the well-known association of child gender and aggression would suggest that negative behaviours such as aggression are more strongly exhibited in boys than in girls.

With respect to parenting, good parenting practices are expected to result in improvements in children's outcomes, while punishing behaviours such as yelling or physical punishment are expected to have negative effects. In keeping with the reports of psychologists, the presence of mental illness in a parent, and depression in particular, is expected to have a deleterious effect on children. Also in keeping with psychologists' expectations, caregiver gender is not expected to be an important precursor of children's outcomes.

Family structure-related variables are expected to affect children's outcomes. An intact, biological family is expected to improve children's outcomes as is an increase in supervision as measured by the parent-child ratio. Household income and an adequate income are also expected to result in improvements in the lives of children.

The preceding section dealt with theoretical formulations regarding the best interests of children, leading to the development of a model that will test not only the factors that produce variation in children's outcomes but also the mechanisms by which these outcomes are produced. I now turn to the empirical aspects of this test, including a description of the data from Statistics Canada's National Longitudinal Survey of Children and Youth, the methods used, and the results obtained.

Data from the National Longitudinal Survey
of Children and Youth

This part of the analysis uses the National Longitudinal Survey of Children and Youth (NLSCY) to examine the predictors of behavioural, educational, and health outcomes in children. The NLSCY is a combined cross-sectional and prospective longitudinal survey of children, designed to be nationally representative, that gathers information on a wide variety of attributes of the children and their environment. The first collection of data for the NLSCY took place from December 1994 to April 1995, and the longitudinal portion has been re-surveyed approximately every two years since.[1] This analysis uses the first four such surveys: all that were available from Statistics Canada at the time of analysis. The data was analysed in the Statistics Canada Regional Data Centre located at the University of Calgary, since both the variables used in the analysis and longitudinal sample are not released to the public by Statistics Canada in order to ensure confidentiality for respondents. Access to this data was only granted after an application to Statistics Canada, which was peer-reviewed before approval to the full NLSCY dataset was granted. The initial survey involved 22,831 children, of whom 16,903 were earmarked for follow-up (longitudinal) surveys until the age of 25. The data used in this analysis was gathered from questions asked to a single person determined by Statistics Canada to be the Person Most Knowledgeable (PMK), most frequently the mother. The full sample, containing as many as four observations per child, included more than 20,102 children. Since the behavioural measures that are used as dependent variables in this analysis were only asked about children between the ages of 4 and 11 years, the sample was limited to children of these ages, leaving 9,789 individual children (before weighting).

The number of children in any given model varies, since any missing values for a child at a given cycle resulted in the case being dropped from the analysis through a process known as list-wise deletion. Missing values happen when respondents do not answer a question for a variety of reasons: they do not know the answer, they refuse to answer, or they don't feel the question applies to them. When any of the data on a case is missing, that case is dropped from the analysis. In some surveys, called simple probability sample surveys, a sample can be used in a straightforward way since each case has the same probability of being selected into the sample. The NLSCY is not a simple probability sample, but a stratified sample, that is, the random sampling takes place only within the smallest division being surveyed. For example, a survey might be divided into provinces, then municipalities, then areas within the municipality where the residents are randomly chosen. In other words, a child has a different chance of being chosen for the survey depending on where the child lives. To compensate for the survey design, Statistics Canada provides variables that weight each child for each cycle to compensate for different rates of sampling in some regions. The weights are given by each child for a given cycle, and the Stata software allows only one set of weights to be applied per child. In order to proceed with the model, the cross-sectional weights given for Cycle 4, divided by the average weight, were used for this purpose, since this allowed the most cases to be used. Hence the analysis will be representative of the population of Canadian children aged 4 to 11 years at the time that Cycle 4 was gathered, that is, late in the year 2000 or early 2001. Since Cycle 4 did not keep track of children from previous cycles who were not present in Cycle 4, many cases could not be weighted, resulting in the loss of more children from the dataset.

Method of Analysis for NLSCY Variables

Many of the key variables of interest in this study were measured by summated rating scales. A summated rating scale combines the results of many questions to form a single indicator. This technique is often used in social science because the combined answers to multiple questions are more reliable, more precise, and reduce the measurement error of a given concept, compared to a single question (Spector 1992). It happens that the measures created in this way were distributed non-normally in a manner that is best represented by a gamma distribution. Many statistical models do not allow use of the gamma distribution. Further, the data is a longitudinal sample where each child was surveyed several times approximately every two years. For these kinds of surveys, when conducted on people, a measure will frequently have significant correlations with the previous measure from the last cycle, a phenomenon called autocorrelation. A technique that accommodates the special needs of these data – gamma distribution, longitudinal sample, and autocorrelation – is panel regression[2] as implemented in the statistical software package Stata. This technique also allowed a transformation of the predicted values to their natural logarithm.[3]

Cluster Analysis

In order to test for the existence of the selectivity causal mechanism, the parents were divided into three groups according to parenting characteristics. This was accomplished using the statistical technique of cluster analysis, which allocates like cases into a specified number of groups according to scores along given variables. This technique was used to group the Persons Most Knowledgeable (PMKs) with respect to their parenting ability in Cycle 1 into three groups: those with the best parenting characteristics, those in the middle, and those with the worst. The group assignment in the first cycle or survey was then used to see if it was significant in explaining children's outcomes, after controlling for more proximate variables such as parenting behaviours. This method was used in order to test the selectivity hypothesis. In other words, if parents can be categorized at the start of the survey, and if these categories explain outcomes for children, then there is evidence for the selectivity mechanism discussed above.

Description of Variables

Outcome Measures

All behavioural outcome measures are summated rating scales asked of the PMK. While this person could in theory be anyone who has daily contact with the child, this analysis will treat the PMK as the main parental or caregiver figure. *Hyperactivity* is the degree to which the child is inattentive or hyperactive. *Pro-social behaviour* measures the degree to which the child is helpful or comforting to other children. *Emotional disorder* measures the degree to which the child is unhappy, worried, nervous, or tense. *Aggression,* or conduct disorder, measures the degree to which the child physically assaults other children. *Indirect aggression* measures the degree to which a child disrupts relationships of someone he or she is angry with. *Property Offences* measures the degree to which a child will destroy his or her belongings or the belongings of others. The health outcome is an estimation of the *child's overall health* by the PMK. Similarly, the educational outcome is an estimation of the *child's overall school performance* by the PMK.

Mediating/Endogenous Variables

The variables which theoretically affect child outcomes, but which are also affected by some of the same variables as the child outcomes, are called mediating or intervening or endogenous variables. These are the variables through which the strain mechanism operates. The parental behaviour measures in this analysis are summated rating scales, again derived from questions asked of the PMK about interactions with the child. *Positive Interaction* is the degree to which the parent praises, laughs, or plays with the child. *Consistency* is the degree to which the child is unable to get away with behaviour, that is, consistency in discipline. *Depression* in the PMK is a summated rating scale representing the degree to which the PMK feels depressed, that everything is an effort, or that he or she could not shake off the blues. *Yell* is the frequency of the PMK yelling, scolding, or raising his or her voice at the child. *Spank* is the degree to which physical punishment is used on the child.

Independent or Exogenous Variables

Variables which affect child outcomes but which are not affected by the other variables in the model are called independent or exogenous variables. *Child's age* was derived by taking the child's actual age at the time of the interview in months and dividing by 12, a slightly different and more precise measure than the nominal age in years used to limit the sample. *Child gender* was male (51 per cent of the sample) or female. *PMK education* was measured in years and ranged from zero to 20. *PMK gender* was male (8 per cent of the sample) or female. *Intact family* was defined as a family of continuously married biological parents (70 per cent of the sample). *Supervision* was measured as the parent-child ratio, that is, the number of parents divided by the number of children. The base 10 logarithm of household income was used as a measure of *household income* since income was not normally distributed. *Income adequacy* was where income was deemed as at least lower-middle income, according to the Statistics Canada criteria. *Custody change* was derived by examining changes in marital status and changes in the caregiver, to see, in the event of relationship dissolution, which parent retained care of the child. There are three possible values: no change, a custody change from previous cycles to the mother, and a custody change to the father. Since this variable measures changes from one cycle to the next, all the values for custody are missing for the first cycle. The *previous value* of each outcome is explicitly included in the model to ensure that all results control for the expected correlations of previous measures of each outcome. In other words, the changes attributed to each variable are net of the previous behaviour, health, or education of the child.

Results

The detailed results for the models estimating the effects of parents and family on children through the direct and selectivity causal mechanisms are shown in Appendix B (p. 91).

Characteristics of the Child

RESILIENCY

The most prominent result is that previous measures of child outcomes are, by far, the best predictors of future outcomes. Note that the previous measure is the measure of the child's outcome from the previous cycle, usually about two years previous. This finding, that the previous measure is the strongest predictor of future measures, is consistent and strong for all measures of children's outcomes with the exception of aggression, where the effect of the previous measure is surpassed only slightly by supervision as a predictor. These models show that by the time a child reaches elementary school age, traits related to behaviour, health, and school performance, while not fixed, are nonetheless resilient to change. Children's success in areas measured here are therefore resilient, while difficulties are challenging to overcome.

CHILD CHARACTERISTICS

These models show that a child's age and sex have significant effects on his or her behaviour, health, and school performance. Specifically, as a child ages, his or her pro-social behaviour and overall health improves and the tendency to destroy property decreases. With respect to gender, boys fare worse on all measures where there is a significant effect for gender except on indirect aggression, for which girls exhibit a much greater propensity than boys. Boys have greater hyperactivity, less pro-social behaviour, more aggression, commit more property offences, and have worse overall health as rated by their caregivers. In general, the age of the child appears to improve child outcomes and being a boy lowers them, except for indirect aggression.

PARENTAL CHARACTERISTICS

Parenting behaviours, controlling for the other variables in the model, have important effects on children's outcomes. Verbal punishment – the tendency to yell, scold, or raise one's voice – appears to have the strongest effects on children's behaviour of all the parental character- istics. It appears to produce a strong negative effect on all children's behavioural outcomes, although it also appears to have a small posi- tive effect on the parent's rating of overall child health. Nevertheless, overall, verbal punishment seems to be a very negative characteristic in terms of its effect on children's behaviour the strongest worsening factor. The second most important characteristic in terms of the mag- nitude of its direct effect on children appears to be the frequency of physical punishment. Physical punishment appears to have no benefi- cial effects and strong negative effects on children's behaviour, similar in magnitude of effect to yelling. On the other hand, behaviours asso- ciated with good parenting practices – consistency and positive inter- action – have beneficial effects on children's outcomes but to a lesser degree than the negative parental behaviours of yelling and spanking, making these the third most important parental behaviours with respect to child behavioural outcomes. Depression in a caregiver appears to have a negative effect on most child outcomes, except pro- social behaviour and school performance: no positive outcomes were associated with this characteristic. The gender of the PMK had no effect in these models on any of the children's outcomes, although only roughly 8 per cent of the PMKs were men in this sample. The variable measuring pre-existing, overall parental characteristics which catego- rized parents into three groups – those with the best parental charac- teristics, those with the worst, and a middle group appeared to have no effect on children's outcomes after controlling for the more tempo- rally proximate parental behaviours and characteristics. Thus, the selectivity causal mechanism does not appear to be supported by the evidence from these models.

FAMILY CHARACTERISTICS

Family characteristics had important consequences for children, even after controlling for parental and child characteristics. An intact, bio- logical family, for example, appears to provide reduced hyperactivity in children, as well as being one of the few explanatory variables that have an effect on school performance with no significant negative effects. The intact biological family also appears, on average, to have an effect similar to the difference between having a PMK with four more years of education: a university degree versus a high school diploma. Another structural effect of the family, increased supervision (operationalized as the parent-to-child ratio) also has beneficial effects for children, with substantively important reductions in the propensity for aggression and property destruction. Increased supervision, on the other hand, was also associated with an increase in children's hyperactivity. Increases in the log of household income had only positive effects for all outcomes and were statistically significant for improvements in hyperactivity, emotional disorder, overall health, and – especially – the tendency to destroy property. The log of household income was substantively the most important effect on overall health, except for the previous measure of the child's overall health. It should be noted, however, that these effects require a tenfold increase in household income, something not easily achievable by social policy. For example, for every tenfold increase in household income there is an expected 43 per cent reduction in the property offense scale for a child (the propensity to destroy property). Having an adequate income was found to be associated with a reduction in emotional disorder for the children in this study. Changes in custody were found to have deleterious effects for this sample of children, with assignment of custody to the mother increasing emotional disorder and custody to the father associated with an increase in children's hyperactivity. It should be noted that the number of cases with a custody assignment to the father in this sample is small, and several effects (both good and bad) were not found to be statistically significant even though they could be substantially important. The same comments apply to the effects of having a male PMK. Hence, more research on this particular subset of the population of children seems to be warranted.

The Strain Model

The purpose of these models is to test the intervening or strain causal mechanism; that is, to see if there is an effect of the exogenous variables on parental behaviour or attributes which in turn affect children's outcomes through strain on the parents. All of these models of indirect effects have been constructed so that a negative coefficient indicates a beneficial effect: the positive interaction and consistency variables were reverse coded for this purpose. The detailed results for the strain models are contained in Appendix B (p. 93).

EFFECTS OF CAREGIVER CHARACTERISTICS

The results for the models predicting parenting practices indicate that indirect mechanisms may be at play in the creation of children's outcomes. For example, caregivers with higher education appear to have higher consistency in discipline, more positive interaction, use less physical discipline, and report less depression than those with lower levels of education. Education can be thought of as a factor that reduces strain on parents or increases their ability to cope. Comparing the results of these effects with the direct effects of PMK education on children's outcomes, the main mechanism for the effects of PMK education appears to be through strain: education appears to have a beneficial effect on parenting and parental mental health, which in turn results in better child outcomes. In contrast to parental education, the effect of parental gender appears to be through the strain mechanism only, favouring male caregivers who report less depression and yell less at their children. This finding in favour of male PMKs should be regarded with some caution, as the proportion of male PMKs is only about 8 per cent. Since there is no population data for Canadian caregivers on these measures – let alone male caregivers – it is difficult to ascertain if these men are different from the Canadian population.

EFFECTS OF FAMILY STRUCTURE ON PARENTS

Family structure has significant effects on parental characteristics and behaviour in addition to the direct effects on children's outcomes noted above. Intact, biological families according to these models are associated with improved parental consistency in discipline as well as reduced parental depression. On the other hand, intact families appear to verbally and physically punish their children more frequently than do other families, which in turn correlates with deficits for children. Supervision, operationalized as the parent-to-child ratio, has a beneficial effect on both verbal and physical punishment, as well as a substantially large beneficial effect on positive interaction of parents with their children. Supervision however, appears to deteriorate consistent discipline, an unanticipated effect.

EFFECTS OF HOUSEHOLD INCOME ON PARENTS

The logarithm of household income had significant indirect effects on children's outcomes. Not surprisingly, a tenfold increase in household income was associated with a substantial, significant decrease in caregiver depression. Specifically, for every tenfold increase in household

income there was an expected 53 per cent decrease in the scale measuring caregiver depression, controlling for the other variables in the
model. Moreover, increasing the base 10 logarithm of household
income was also associated with expected improvements in parental
consistency and physical punishment, as well as with an unanticipated
worsening effect on positive parental interaction. An adequate household income was associated with beneficial effects on the frequency of
verbal and physical punishment.

EFFECTS OF A CHANGE IN CUSTODY ON PARENTS
A change in custody to the father is associated with improvements in
parental consistency as well as a reduction in the frequency of physical punishment. These results are unanticipated and should probably
be viewed with some caution pending further research since the proportion of these cases (father caregiver) is small.

Causal Mechanisms

These models, although designed to model variables which explain
variation in children's outcomes, were also designed to test three
causal mechanisms: direct effects of the family on children; effects of
strain on the family on children (the intervening model); and a selectivity mechanism in which parents were categorized at the first cycle
of data collection to see if this pre-existing category was more important than more proximate behaviours. The empirical test resulting
from the application of NLSCY data to these models is consistent with
only two of these mechanisms; the selectivity model was not supported. On the other hand, the family appears to affect children both
directly and through its impact on parenting practices.

Discussion

The most prominent finding of the first investigation in this work
found that the gender of the parent plays a key role in the determination of child custody in Canadian divorces. Given the emphasis in
Canadian law on the best interests of the child as the overriding criterion for making these decisions, and the common social science
finding that gender per se is rarely a good predictor of individual suit-
ability for most social roles, it left unanswered the question of whether
or not parental gender is aligned with other characteristics that *are*

demonstrably in children's best interests. The results of this most recent analysis suggest that parental gender is not a good predictor – in fact not a predictor at all – of any of the child outcomes examined here; that is, behavioural, educational, or health outcomes. Thus, there appears to be a disconnect between the theoretical criterion of custody determinations – best interests – and what actually plays out in the context of the justice system. The ideological roots of this discrepancy appear to derive from the legally influential theories of the best interests of the child as presented by writers such as Goldstein, Freud, and Solnit (1986). While this is a central finding of this research, there are other findings here that have import for the custody decision-making process.

As expected, children's behavioural, educational, and health characteristics are resilient for this age group: that is, the best predictor of these characteristics is the previous measure for them. This supports the contention of authors such as Gottfredson and Hirschi (1990) that ingrained traits, which they collectively label under the umbrella of low self control, are a main predictor of antisocial or deviant behaviour. Conversely, a child with established positive behaviours is resilient to many negative influences. Nevertheless, there remain important effects from parenting practices and family structure, even after controlling for resiliency. For example, while psychologists doing custody evaluations already deem parenting practices to be an important consideration in assessing the fitness of a parent, this analysis provides information on some specific behaviours and reports on their consequences, in particular the relatively stronger effect of punishing behaviours compared to more positive parenting practices. Thus, the relative importance of punishing behaviours – yelling and physical punishment – is something that could be incorporated into custody evaluation frameworks. The finding that depression in a caregiver has a negative impact on children – suspected by most psychologists evaluating custody – is confirmed, but is also shown to be affecting a wide range of outcomes, pointing to the need for more population-based research on other psychological conditions and their relative impact on the children of people with these conditions. The substantial direct impact of supervision on aggression and the property offence scale, as well as the indirect effects of higher parent-child ratios through strain on parents, has an important bearing on criminogenic research, as well as for custody determination. To date, both judges and psychologists have been reluctant to split siblings between parents, so generally all the children go to one parent or the other, with the rationale that the best interests of children is served by keeping the children together. This finding suggests, other factors held constant, that split custody may have some benefits that were previously unsuspected. One custody expert suggests that in some situations the 'benefits of split custody outweigh the drawbacks' (Warshak 1992:199). Like all social science findings, more confirmatory evidence needs to be gathered before large changes in custody assignment can be made confidently. Nevertheless, split custody may be less harmful than once thought. Moreover, the presence of grandparents in the home might be a benefit for children, although this research did not specifically control for the effects of extended family.

For criminological research, the significance is that aggression is due only partly from the single-mother family structure: more child aggression seems to come from the parent-to-child ratio than the non-intact family per se, although this still plays a part. Moreover, the finding that girls are more likely than boys to engage in indirect aggression is consistent with previous findings (Gorman-Smith 2003) and could inform the growing area of interest in gender and criminology and the study of female aggression in general. Household income, as expected, had a positive effect on children's outcomes but the effect appears to mostly indirect through reducing strain on parents, and requires very large changes in income (effects were measured in tenfold increases) to make important differences. So, while household income has significant effects for children's outcomes, these effects may not provide the greatest point of leverage for improving children's lives upon divorce, compared to, say, choosing the parent who is less likely to use physical punishment or yell at the children. This is not to say that household income has no relevance, only to place the effects of income in perspective with other considerations since very large changes in household income are difficult to achieve through child support awards. Further, child support awards are limited by the economic situation of the non-custodial parent, which means that the poorest families are at the greatest disadvantage in this respect upon divorce.

A change in custody was expected to affect children in a negative way, and this was the case in the model for direct effects; however, the models showed a significant indirect effect for custody awarded to the father, counter to expectations. These results could be due to a number of possibilities; for example, fathers with especially good parenting characteristics may be more likely to retain custody of their children, or these fathers may be self-selected in some other way that produces better outcomes. This result should be regarded with some caution for this reason, and because the number of male caregivers in this analysis was small compared to the number of females. In any case, this finding does not support the current strong gender preference evident in custody determinations in Canada.

These results highlight a number of measures which can now be empirically associated with the best interests of the child in terms of behavioural, educational, and health outcomes. It is hoped that this contribution will pave the way to establishing concrete measures of a child's 'best interests,' and further work that explores what factors are available to improve the lives of children, especially the children of divorce.

The findings of this analysis, while able to comment on the effects of family, child characteristics, parental characteristics, parenting, and income on child outcomes, were not able to examine the impact of child support on children, although household income clearly has an impact, even if large changes in income are involved.

The next chapter looks at the impact of child support on household income, as well as the relative variability of child support compared with such factors as the income of the payor and the number of children in the household.

APPENDIX B

Note that improvements are indicated by a negative coefficient for all explanatory variables in all models. The effect coefficients in these models are exponential; that is, the marginal effects are obtained by raising e to the power of the effect coefficient. The models were first estimated without the parenting and parental cluster variables, and with only one measure of household income in order to demonstrate that both measures of income had separate effects, and to ensure that the parental cluster variables did not appreciably affect the effects exerted by the variables measuring parenting behaviours, since the parental clusters were constructed from parental characteristics. It appears there is an effect for income adequacy that does not diminish the effect for log of household income.

Table B1 Models predicting children's outcomes (full models)

		Hyper-activity	Pro-social behaviour	Emotional disorder	Aggression	Indirect aggression	Property offences	Overall health	School performance
	Previous measure	0.21 ***	0.19 ***	0.32 ***	0.41 ***	0.38 ***	0.90 ***	0.29 ***	0.27 ***
Child	Age	-0.01	-0.03 ***	0.01	-0.01	-0.03	-0.16 ***	-0.01	0.00
	Boy	0.24 ***	0.24 ***	-0.01	0.25 ***	-0.37 ***	0.44 ***	0.01	0.06 ***
Parent	Yell (verbal)	0.17 ***	-0.06 **	0.16 ***	0.28 ***	0.28 ***	0.39 ***	-0.02 *	0.01
	Spank (physical)	0.08 ***	0.03	0.05 *	0.27 ***	0.11 *	0.34 ***	0.01	0.03
	Positive interaction	-0.02 **	-0.09 ***	-0.01	-0.04 ***	-0.01	-0.09 **	-0.01 ***	-0.01 *
	Consistency	-0.05 ***	-0.01	-0.04 ***	-0.08 ***	-0.10 ***	-0.10 ***	-0.01 **	-0.01
	PMK depression	0.04 ***	-0.01	0.05 ***	0.07 ***	0.04 ***	0.05 *	0.02 ***	0.00
	PMK education	-0.02 *	0.00	0.02 *	0.00	0.00	-0.02	-0.01 ***	-0.02 ***
	PMK gender (male)	0.01	0.06	0.09	-0.16	0.17	-0.30	-0.03	0.00
	PMK cluster (0) (ref.)†								
	PMK cluster (1)	0.01	0.01	0.05	-0.11	0.04	0.10	0.00	0.01
	PMK cluster (2)	0.07	0.04	-0.03	-0.02	0.11	0.13	-0.02	0.04
Family	Intact family	-0.13 ***	0.00	-0.05	0.07	-0.09	-0.16	0.02	-0.08 ***
	Supervision	0.12 **	-0.02	0.03	-0.47 ***	-0.10	-0.39 ***	0.03	0.02
	Log10(income)	-0.21 *	-0.05	-0.29 ***	-0.11	-0.08	-0.57 ***	-0.14 ***	-0.05
	Adequate income	-0.05	0.02 *	-0.16 ***	-0.06	-0.05	-0.21	-0.02	-0.03
Custody change	No change (ref.)								
	Custody to mother	-0.03	-0.07	0.13 ***	0.02	0.05	0.05	0.04	-0.01
	Custody to father	0.24 **	0.03	0.22	0.32	-0.33	0.19	0.01	-0.03
	No. of children	5,076	4,921	5,073	4,855	4,525	4,806	5,093	2,778
	No. of observations	13,300	12,800	13,288	11,153	10,379	11,077	13,356	5,564

* p<.05; ** p <.01; *** p<.001 (two-tailed tests).
Note that negative coefficients mean beneficial effects for all variables.
†Parents were clustered into three categories on pre-existing parenting characteristics to test the selectivity model of causation.

Table B2 Models estimating effects of exogenous variables on endogenous variables (strain model)

	Positive interaction(r)	Consistency(r)	PMK depression	Yell	Spank
PMK education	-0.02 ***	-0.03 ***	-0.05 ***	0.00	-0.01 *
PMK gender (male)	0.07	0.02	-0.19 *	-0.03 *	0.01
Intact family	0.00	-0.10 ***	-0.21 ***	0.02 *	0.06 ***
Supervision	-0.24 ***	0.07 **	-0.04	-0.05 ***	-0.07 ***
Adequate income	-0.07 ***	0.02 ***	-0.01	-0.03 *	-0.05 *
Log10 (income)	0.12 *	-0.12 *	-0.76 ***	-0.02	-0.16 ***
No custody change (ref.)					
Custody to mother	0.07	-0.04	0.06	-0.02	-0.02
Custody to father	0.02	-0.16 *	0.14	-0.03	-0.10 *
No. of children	8,301	8,174	8,518	8,281	8,280
No. of observations	20,226	19,829	20,757	20,175	20,175

* p<.05; ** p <.01; *** p<.001 (two tailed) tests).
(r) reverse coded compared to previous model.

5 The Effect of Child Support on Household Income

Perhaps few issues that routinely arise in family law bear the emotionally laden overtones associated with child support. The last chapter focused on the causes of children's outcomes in the hope of providing some elucidation of what empirically represents the best interests of children. Household income was found to affect children's outcomes, both directly and indirectly, although the impact of income is considerably less than that of parenting. Moreover, most of the effect of income is through the logarithm of household income, meaning that household income must increase tenfold to attain the indicated effect. Thus, the effect of income – emphasized in family law as being the key factor affecting children – should be kept in perspective with respect to its relative importance. This section carries the investigation further by examining the effect of child support on household income. In order to accomplish this task, I will first review some issues related to child support before providing details of the data used to conduct this empirical investigation, the results obtained, and the implications for policy.

While state-ordered support of family members has been the subject of legislation since at least the time of Elizabeth I (An Act for the Relief of the Poor 1601), the issue of child support was most prominently brought to the public's attention in its current context in the latter half of the 1980s, following the publication of *The Divorce Revolution* (Weitzman 1985). In one of the most cited social science works of its time, Weitzman claimed that, after divorce, men's standard of living shot dramatically upward while women's plummeted even more dramatically downward. This work, more than any other, provided fuel for the contention that divorce, and in particular low awards of child support, were an important cause of children's poverty, cited in many of the documents relating to the development of the Canadian child support guidelines (Millar and Gauthier 2002). The image of divorced men living a lifestyle depicted in beer commercials while their former wives and children languished in poverty was understandably offensive to the public, and a dramatic change in policy soon ensued, with an accompanying social stigma of 'deadbeat dad' to the facilitator of his own children's poverty. In Canada, provinces reacted to this by creating departments dedicated to the collection of child support, and, in 1997, in conjunction with the federal government, implemented presumptive child support guidelines which specify the amount of child support that must be ordered pursuant to divorce in Canada.[1]

All of this might well be justified if the concerns about the effects of child support on children's poverty were true. However, Weitzman's work was later found to be numerically incorrect (Peterson 1996); that is, the dramatic differences between the living standards of men and women after divorce were largely due to numerical errors in her calculations. After the errors were accounted for, there remained a difference in living standards that favoured men, but by a much slimmer margin than was first alleged. Moreover, Weitzman incorrectly assumed, as has most subsequent empirical research, that non-custodial parents have no costs related to the children while the custodial parent bears 100 per cent of the cost of raising children after divorce. This assumption has also proven to be incorrect (Braver and O'Connell 1998; Fabricius and Braver 2004; Fabricius, Braver, and Deneau 2003; Finnie 1997), although the magnitude of these costs is under-researched. In retrospect, it strains credulity to understand how researchers could make this assumption when most non-custodial parents remain involved in their children's lives, with significant attendant costs. These findings, that the research leading to significant policy initiatives related to child support was flawed, received far less public exposure than the original research and no change in policy has arisen as a result.

Given this context, it is perhaps not surprising that the Canadian child support guidelines, while providing the benefit of a consistent guideline for support calculations and substantially increasing support payments,[2] had several potential problems according to one of the guidelines' developers (Finnie 1997). The guidelines altered the tax treatment of support in such a way as to substantially increase taxation[3] on non-custodial parents while reducing on average the potential size of awards. The guidelines, as implemented, substantially increased amounts payable by low-income payors (compared to earlier proposals) while introducing a category of 'special expenses' that were included in the formulation of the guidelines, double-counting these expenses. That is, the guidelines already accounted for these expenses, but this category allowed them to be added in again. Moreover, there is no requirement that the payments be spent on the children, no allowance for the costs incurred by the non-custodial parent,[4] and no adjustments for tax credits related to the children. Aside from these criticisms offered by Finnie, another challenge to dealing with child support is the variation of income over time.

The issue of child support and its variation over time have recently been decided by the Supreme Court of Canada with its decision on retroactive support in four cases rendered together: *D.B.S. v. S.R.G.*; *L.J.W. v. T.A.R.*; *Henry v. Henry*; and *Hiemstra v. Hiemstra* (2006). In that judgment, the court found retroactive support was justified in two of the cases but not in the other two. The judgment, referring most notably to the previous case of *Willick v. Willick* (1994), suggests that the amount of support should be adjusted upward retroactive to income increases where there has been a significant increase in the payor's income. The court had to wrestle with this issue since income varies regularly whereas court orders do not; some guidance was needed on how to manage this variation.

The variation in income brings to light the inappropriateness of the courts as an institution to manage child support since family situations and household income change frequently, but courts are designed to handle infrequently occurring events of significant import and to make a determination that is designed to stand for many years. Moreover, great expense, both for the individuals involved and the state, is associated with court intervention. Even an out of court agreement can entail significant expense and effort. While decisions of custody are infrequent and somewhat permanent, management of the ongoing assessment of the amount of child support and its collection are activities that the courts are ill-equipped to deal with. Conditions associated with the determination of child support amounts, such as income and family configuration, change at least annually. Yet neither the court process nor the guidelines provide for regular changes in the amount payable, which allows a number of unfair situations to develop, including less support than could be provided when the payor's income increases and unfairly high support payments on the behalf of the payor when his or her income decreases.

It is doubly difficult for the payor to achieve downward adjustments in support when his or her ability to pay has decreased, since the courts are oriented to increasing, not decreasing, support. Further, the downward change in income must have established itself as permanent, so arrears are likely to accrue while the payor waits for his or her day in court. Income is a moving target, sometimes incurring extreme variation – self-employed individuals sometimes even have negative income. Hence, it seems unrealistic to expect that payments will remain fair for many years without variation. Income tax, for example, is calculated annually; suggesting that income tax should remain constant for many years without variation obviously would be intolerable because of the inherently unfair situations that would inevitably develop. It is only the moral climate, the reduction of payments through inflation, the financially disadvantaged position of non-custodial parents behind on support payments, and the quasi-criminal stigma (see below) associated with being a 'deadbeat' that has enabled this situation to be sustained in cases of child support where it would be unsustainable in the case of income tax.

The development of a quasi-criminal legal environment for the collection of child support is something rarely discussed in the literature, and yet it is relevant to the context of both children's outcomes and the legal policy implications related to child support. While a full investigation of the effects of this regime is beyond the scope of this inquiry, the proliferation of the law of divorce and corollary family issues has developed certain quasi-criminal characteristics, including the incarceration of those in arrears in their support payments. Because of the greater consequences of criminal law to its subjects, and the imbalance of power between the state and individual, criminal law requires a stricter adherence to procedures that restrict the powers of state actors, a much stricter standard of proof, and a guarantee of legal representation. The enforcement of support collection displays many of the features of criminal law although maintaining a non-criminal status, which could be characterized as quasi-criminal (Freiberg 2006). This quasi-criminal status allows the actions of the enforcement agency and courts to elude the procedural and substantive protections normally afforded individuals facing criminal or criminal-like penalties.

Enforcement action is accomplished through provincial enforcement agencies, such as the Family Responsibility Office in Ontario, and the courts. Provincial enforcement agencies employ a variety of coercive actions to obtain payment, including restriction of drivers' licenses, suspension of licenses to practice certain professions, reporting the debtor to credit bureaus, registering liens against real and personal property, seizure of federal and provincial funds owing to the debtor, garnishment of wages, and cancellation and denial of passports, among other possible actions. Although some of these actions are also available to private debt collectors, most of the actions taken by provincial enforcement agencies take virtually no effort on the part of the collector since most provincial maintenance enforcement agencies have electronic interfaces with the other government agencies involved: the actions can be triggered automatically upon given non-payment conditions or at the touch of a button. Hence, these enforcement agencies are at a great advantage compared to ordinary (private) debt collections agencies, both in terms of the types of coercive actions available to them and the ease of taking commonly available actions. Court enforcement commonly takes the form of a default or committal hearing, where debtors are compelled to appear before a judge who could order a variety of remedies, the most severe of which is a prison term. The resulting incarcerations, to provincial reformatories for non-payment of support, have become a routine occurrence in Canada.

The lack of legal protections for those facing prosecution for default of support payments is also supported by the powerful social stigma of 'deadbeat dad,'[5] which renders those behind in support payments vulnerable to the many informal punishments that society inflicts on its most despised classes. This stigma may have a strength similar to that of criminality; in a recent plan to share oil revenues with the citizens of Alberta, the provincial government issued cheques to all residents, even if they owed income tax, student loans, or other government debt. The payments were denied or diverted only to those incarcerated and to those who owe child support (Government of Alberta 2005), suggesting that the stigma associated with support arrears (being a 'deadbeat dad') is similar to that of incarceration, at least in Alberta. This could suggest that being a 'deadbeat dad' carries a greater stigma than simple criminality, since a minority of sentencing for criminal offences involves incarceration. Such a punitive approach to the collection of support may facilitate payments, but given that household income is only one factor – and not the most substantive – among many, it may not be in children's best interests to focus solely on support enforcement as the main mechanism with which to improve children's lives.

Since the empirical results of the previous chapter suggest that income is a concern, if a secondary one, in the formation of children's outcomes,[6] I now turn to the issue of the effect of child support on household income.

Hypotheses

The research undertaken in this section investigates the degree to which support payments reflect the income of the payor and the family situation of the payee, as well as the proportions of household income represented by support. Since the payment of child support is formally predicated on the payor's income and the number of children of the marriage, it is expected that there is at least a moderate degree of correlation with the guiding principles of support awards. Hence, the expectation is that income will be related to the amount of child support paid and the number of dependent children, or, more specifically, the Statistics Canada 40/30 Scale, derived from the number of dependent children, will be a predictor of the amount of child support received. Further, the regional differences in child support payments should not be significant since the awards were derived from the same basic formula for all provinces, except Quebec, which of all the provinces would be the only one that should show major deviation by province. Since court decisions are infrequent and income varies, at least annually, it is expected that support payments paid and received are more stable than income. Finally, the introduction of the guidelines in May 1997 should show a difference in child support awards since this was the first appearance of a nation-wide child support scheme.

Data

The Survey of Labour and Income Dynamics (SLID) is a Statistics Canada survey conducted yearly that collects information on household labour, income, and expenses representative of Canadians living in the 10 provinces, with the exception of native reserves and institutions, up to the year 2002. Although the dataset available from Statistics Canada contains data dating from 1993, including information on support payments received, information for support payments paid is available only from 1999. The data surveyed 256,744 households, 3,121 of which received support over the 10-year period and 2,347 of which paid support from 1999.[7]

These data have many limitations which constrain the types of analyses that can be performed and the conclusions which can be drawn from those analyses. Perhaps the most important limitation is that the households paying and receiving support are not connected. This inability to connect paying and receiving households constrains the analysis to separate considerations of support paid and support received, with no attendant analysis of whether the amounts paid or received are appropriate from the point of view of the child support guidelines. The guidelines require information from both the paying household (income) and the receiving household (number of children of the former marriage). Moreover, the 'fairness' of the awards cannot be examined, that is, the effect on the receiving household compared to the effect on the paying household. The data have further limitations other than the inability to connect paying and receiving households: there is no indication whether the support received is legally deemed to be child support or spousal support, whether it is paid or received. For this analysis, the assumption is made that support received for households with dependent children is for child support. Also, the data do not reveal which children the support payments are associated with. Because of these limitations, amounts of support paid and support received are analysed separately, with a focus on the number of children in the household for households that receive support, and a focus on household income for those that pay support.

Of the 5,434 households that either received or paid support, only 34, or less than 1 per cent, both paid and received support (see Table 5.1). Of these, 11, or roughly a third, paid more than they received. Because of the small number of households in this sample that both paid and received support, no separate analysis of this sub-sample was performed.

Variables

Support paid is the total amount of support paid by everyone in the household. *Support received* is the total amount of support received by everyone in the household. *Household income* is the total household income. The *number of dependent children* was derived by counting the number of individuals in the household under the age of 25 attending school in households with more than one more person. *Region* is

Table 5.1 Number of cases where support is paid and received

		Received support		Total
		No	Yes	
Paid support	No	251,310	3,087	254,397
	Yes	2,313	34	2,347
	Total	253,623	3,121	256,744

Table 5.2 The Statistics Canada 40/30 Scale

No. of children	40/30 Scale
1	0.4
2	0.7
3	1.0
4	1.3
5	1.6
6	1.9

recorded as Atlantic, Quebec, Ontario, Prairie, or British Columbia. *Guidelines* indicates the guidelines are in effect, that is if the year is greater than 1997 (the Canadian child support guidelines were introduced on 1 May 1997).[8] The 40/30 Scale is directly derived from the number of dependent children, as shown in Table 5.2, and is the scale used to estimate differences in household costs between custodial and non-custodial households for the purposes of the guidelines.

Descriptive Statistics

Table 5.3 describes the relationship between the number of cases where support was received and the number of dependent children. Note that in the analyses that follow, support receipt models are limited to cases where the number of dependent children is greater than zero.

Table 5.4 shows the mean support payment by region and income category. Note that this table does not control for the number of children involved in the support arrangements, nor was there a distinction between amounts intended for child and spousal support. Note also

Table 5.3. Support by number of dependent children

Number of dependent children	Received support		Total
	No	Yes	
0	163,086	942	164,028
1	37,154	1,106	38,260
2	37,716	837	38,553
3	12,200	182	12,382
4	2,715	41	2,756
5+	753	13	765
Total	253,623	3,121	256,744
Total (kids>0)		2,179	

Table 5.4 Average support paid by income of payor

Region	Overall	Income category			
		$0-24,999	$25-39,999	$40-54,999	$55,000+
Atlantic	$4,653	$2,752	$4,057	$4,926	$10,595
Quebec	$5,306	$3,072	$3,703	$6,021	$9,538
Ontario	$7,073	$4,689	$4,531	$6,254	$10,299
Prairie	$5,774	$3,983	$4,339	$6,273	$8,548
B.C.	$6,164	$4,261	$6,152	$4,873	$8,333
Canada	$6,067	$3,748	$4,386	$5,952	$9,600
N	2,757	657	756	614	730

that the overall (average) amounts are positively skewed; that is, although the income categories are divided into four roughly equal parts (quartiles), the average is much higher than would be suggested by the mid-point of the second and third quartiles.

Nevertheless, there is a clear association between payment and income, although in Ontario, the lowest income quartile has a higher average payment than the second quartile.

Table 5.5 shows the average (mean) support received by region and number of dependent children. The table shows higher amounts of support for households with no dependent children, an unexpected result which cannot be adequately explained without a connection to the households from which the support originates. Where children are

Table 5.5 Average support received by number of dependent children

Region	Overall	Overall with kids	Number of dependent children			
			0	1	2	3+
Atlantic	$4,295	$4,099	$4,953	$3,341	$4,898	$9,403
Quebec	$6,132	$4,851	$8,552	$4,928	$4,799	$7,098
Ontario	$6,343	$5,503	$8,151	$4,901	$5,857	$7,860
Prairie	$4,383	$4,312	$4,581	$3,622	$4,821	$5,341
B.C.	$4,718	$4,105	$6,547	$3,729	$3,780	$4,157
Canada	$5,623	$4,829	$7,458	$4,401	$5,094	$6,808
N	4,579	1,822	935	920	648	254

Table 5.6 Correlations of support amounts with the amount of the previous year

Year	No. children	40/30 Scale	Support received	Support paid	Total income
1994	1.00	1.00	1.00		
1995	0.85	0.85	0.95		
1996	0.82	0.82	0.88		
1997	0.98	0.98	0.94		
1998	0.87	0.87	0.84		
1999	0.73	0.73	0.27		
2000	0.91	0.91	0.67	0.81	0.64
2001	0.83	0.83	0.30	0.80	0.62
2002	0.80	0.80	0.81	0.80	0.63

present, there appears to be a rank order association with the number of children and the amount of support received, with the exception of Quebec, where the average for households with one child is higher than for households with two children. This could be due to variation in the income of the households from which support originates. Table 5.6 shows the autocorrelation of certain values with the previous year's value. The correlation of one year's support with the next allows an exploration of the relative variability of the payor's total household income, the support paid, support received, and the number of dependent children in the payee's household.

A correlation of 1.0 indicates that the support was the same, on average, as the previous year. A correlation of 0.0 indicates that the support in one year bore no relation to the support in the next. Consequently, the correlation values in Table 5.6 can be viewed as a measure of the variability of support from year to year. Note that income shows more variability from year to year than does the support paid. Beginning in 1999, the amount of support received, however, seems to begin to vary a great deal more than previously, possibly due to a delayed effect of the implementation of the guidelines.

The least stable figure, year to year, is income of the payor, which varies considerably more than support paid, while the most stable values are the number of children.

The support received also appears to be stable, with the exception of the period from 1998 to 2001. If incomes, on average, increase over time, this would suggest that support payments would, again on average, drift below the guidelines. Any income changes in addition to overall inflationary trends should exacerbate the discrepancies between income and support paid, with some payors paying far more than what the guidelines would prescribe, given unfavourable changes in financial circumstances, while others paid less upon improved financial success. Stringent enforcement measures may account for the relatively greater stability in support payments made vis-à-vis income, as well as the stability in support received. An examination of the distributions of support paid and received as a fraction of total income of the household shows that the most common proportion of support to income was 0.085 (the mode). In other words, the most common proportion of support to income was about 8.5 per cent of income for both payors and recipients. The fraction of household income, particularly for support payors, is much lower than would be expected by awards dictated by the Canadian child support guidelines. This finding supports the contention that child support is drifting away – on average, lower – from the guidelines as time passes, accounting for the lower than expected amounts of child support as proportion of payors' income. It also suggests that support payments are not, on average, a crucially large proportion of the incomes of support recipients, with the attendant reduction in emphasis for its bearing on the welfare of children.

I now turn to a few simple statistical models developed for this research.

Multivariate Models

Multivariate models, those that estimate the effects of many variables at once, can add greater understanding to the causes of social phenomena, since most social issues have complex social contexts and multiple causes. Although this analysis is far from meeting that ideal of accounting for all important contextual issues, the examination of the independent effects of variables like income and region on support is still of interest. The data limit this investigation to basic parameters such as region, income, and the number of dependent children. Two models were conducted, one for support paid and one for support received, the details of which are provided in Appendix C (p. 107).

The first model, explaining variation in support paid, is restricted to incomes over $20,000, since incomes above that figure vary approximately in a linear fashion to support payments according to the guidelines. There is a significant effect of income (expected) on the support paid; however, the size of the effect is lower than would be expected if all support amounts were in accordance with the child support guidelines: income explains only about 10 per cent of the variation in support paid, controlling for the region of residence. Also, as expected, there is no significant difference in support paid by region except for Quebec, which has its own separate set of child support guidelines. In other words, child support payments behave approximately as expected with respect to region and income. The model also shows that, controlling for income of the payor, residents of Quebec on average pay about $746 less support than do residents of Ontario (the comparison region). These results should be treated with some caution, since the model does not control for the number of dependent children involved in the support arrangement.

Moving to the receiving side of the equation, another model (details also included in Appendix C) was created to show the effect of the Statistics Canada 40/30 Scale, region, and whether the payments were received after the introduction of the guidelines. This model showed significant differences in support received between Ontario and the other regions, except for Quebec; however, this might be explained by average differences in incomes of the payor, which are unknown in this dataset. The introduction of the guidelines appears to have had an effect on the average amount of support received: $660 annually, or about 11 per cent, less than the 32 anticipated (Finnie 1997:84). As expected, the Statistics Canada 40/30 Scale has a significant effect on the amount of support received; however, the relationship appears to be very weak. Overall, the model explains only 0.8 per cent of the variation in support received, much lower than expected if all support receipts were set in accordance with the Canadian child support guidelines.

As noted above, these preceding analyses should be regarded with some caution, since the data do not allow for a connection between paying and receiving households. Nevertheless, it appears that the results seen here support a finding that, although awards may be initially set according to the guidelines, they do not necessarily remain that way. Thus, support awards appear to follow the principle of stare decisis as opposed to maintaining regular adjustments vis-à-vis the guidelines.

Discussion

The foregoing analysis suggests that there are a number of problems with the administration of child support in Canada. Child support has lower variability than income, so that payments for those whose income has increased are likely to be lower than the guidelines suggest, while the opposite is the case for those whose income has decreased. Moreover, timely adjustment of support payments to income should increase, overall, the amount of support available to custodial parents. The amounts of support paid and received are related to the expected determinants of these amounts, but to a much lesser degree than expected. The number of children is not as strongly related to the amount of support received as expected; household income is not as strongly related to the amount of support paid as expected. Further, the amounts paid after the introduction of the guidelines do not show the expected increase in support amounts as a proportion of income, although it did have an upward effect on the amounts paid. The only regional difference in amounts paid is in Quebec, which again has a different set of guidelines compared to the rest of Canada. The guidelines are affecting income in the directions expected, but not to the degree expected.

The incarceration of debtors for non-payment without benefit of many of the protections guaranteed by the Canadian Charter of Rights and Freedoms may represent an inappropriately heavy emphasis on child support collection than is justified by the best interests of the child; it is unlike the protections afforded other kinds of debt (Miller 1997:98). The social benefits from the coercive collection of support may not exceed the costs, when viewed from the perspective of children, whose parental relationships, including those of the non-custodial parents, are an important resource. While I argue this point on the basis of the best interests of the children, the problems of justifying the attenuation of due process in family law can also be argued from the standpoint of parental rights (Hubin 1999).

Finally, the courts are an inappropriate institution for dealing with the administration of family finances pursuant to divorce. Income varies highly over time, and, with it, the ability to pay support. An administration similar to that provided by the Canada Customs and Revenue Service for the collection of tax, which has a greater focus on practical issues than on punishment, seems more appropriate than the current regime with a mandate more aligned with criminal enforcement than civil administration. These issues may be dealt with only partly by the judiciary, although the Supreme Court of Canada is not without agency in suggesting and sometimes ordering reforms in the executive branch of government. Perhaps the greatest barrier to reform in this area will be relinquishing an issue that the courts have been intensely embroiled in, and that has consumed a great deal of judicial thought in the past several decades.

APPENDIX C

Table C1 shows the details of a regression of region and income on child support payments.

Table C1 OLS regression of support paid on income and region where income is between $20,000 and $150,000 per year and support paid is less than $100,000

Variable		B	Beta	SE	P	
Income ($)		0.09	0.33	16.31	0.000	***
Region	Ontario (ref.)					
	Atlantic	-596.90	-0.03	-1.24	0.216	
	Quebec	-745.86	-0.06	-2.59	0.010	**
	Prairies	-234.74	-0.01	-0.67	0.501	
	B.C.	41.58	0.00	0.11	0.910	
Constant		1,974.21		5.77	0.000	
N		2,285				
Adj R2		11%				

*p<.05; **p<.01; ***p<.001.

Table C.2 shows the effects of the Statistics Canada 40/30 Scale, region, and year of the guidelines introduction on support payments received.

Table C2 OLS regression of support received on the Statistics Canada 40/30 Scale, region and guidelines introduction

Variable		B	Beta	SE	p	
SC 40/30 Scale		2,105.18	0.06	710.4	0.003	**
Region	Ontario (ref.)					
	Atlantic	-1,424.94	-0.05	657.7	0.03	*
	Quebec	-513.276	-0.03	425.1	0.227	
	Prairies	-1,215.38	-0.05	497.2	0.015	*
	B.C.	-1353.18	-0.06	499.1	0.007	**
Guidelines		660.2523	0.04	333.1	0.048	*
Constant		3,844.383		539.8	0.000	***
N		2,537				
Adj R2		0.8%				

*p<.05; **p<.01; ***p<.001.

6 Conclusions

This book pulls together several disparate analyses in order to research the area of family law to see if it lives up to its claim of acting in the best interests of children. This approach is not unprecedented: such a bricolage of investigations has been put to good effect in such works as *Street Corner Society* (Whyte 1993[1943]), where separate inquiries into different aspects of a community are assembled in order to give a composite picture of an aspect of society. That is the approach taken here. This approach was necessary because a single dataset was not available that would permit the sort of research dictated by an inquiry into children's best interests and the alignment of the courts to those interests. This research takes the tack of using empirical, population-based measures of children's outcomes to represent children's best interests, and looks at court orders – both 'consent orders' negotiated out of court and orders arrived at pursuant to a trial in court – as part of the same system. Within this context, conclusions regarding custody and support were developed that have policy implications that differ from the current directions of Canadian public policy.

Custody

The journey undertaken by this work began with the observation that the judiciary in Canada has adopted the 'best interests' standard wholeheartedly; the Supreme Court has developed a framework whereby even the Constitution does not apply to decisions involving the best interests standard. Without a definitive set of criteria that defines this supra-constitutional idea of 'best interests,' a condition which describes the current state of family law in Canada, the best interests criteria degenerates into judicial discretion unfettered by any legal constraint save the review of superior courts. This discretion, as the analysis of court-ordered custody decisions demonstrates, has not been exercised at random. The custody data from the Department of Justice illustrate a pronounced reliance on stereotypical notions of gender roles: parental gender is, by far, the most important predictor of custody outcomes. It might be argued that other variables, unmeasured in this analysis, are more determinative in the assignment of custody; however, the model that predicts the custody outcome is a strongly predictive one. Given the strength of the model and the characteristics of predictors like gender, the chances of another predictor being more important (or even substantially rivalling gender) seem slight. Therefore, if we are to save the possibility that custody outcomes are yet in the interests of children, we are left only with the argument that gender serves as a proxy for characteristics that are important for children's welfare or we must abandon the claim that the court has been acting in children's interests. The latter option is the only one supported by the evidence. The models testing the effect of caregiver gender on children's behaviour, health, and school performance indicate there is no direct effect of caregiver gender on these outcomes. The models even suggest a benefit, through an indirect effect that of having a male caregiver but this result should be treated with some caution since the sample contained many more female caregivers than male. Indeed, the argument being made here – one that is strongly supported by empirical evidence – is not that male caregivers are superior, but that gender of a parent or caregiver is a poor indicator of parental fitness. Hence, the judiciary in Canada cannot be said to be acting in children's best interests with respect to the assignment of custody. As the early feminist author Charlotte Perkins Gilman (1998:293 {1898}) wrote, 'not every woman is born with the special qualities and powers needed to take right care of children.' Although the Supreme Court of Canada has declared that the 'best interests' principle overrides any legal principle, it appears as though the constitutional protection against discrimination by gender is congruent with the 'best interests' principle. This should be of some comfort to those arguing for protections of human rights, since the rationalizations for law protecting individuals from discrimination based on categories such as sex appear to be not only philosophically attractive, but also based on solid empirical evidence, at least with respect to the parenting of children.

Ranking the Factors That Affect Children's Interests

This work aims to accomplish more than to simply show that the judiciary has been falling short with respect to acting in children's best interests; it is intended to be a first attempt to provide population-based evidence useful not only to adjudicators, but also to custody evaluators and those concerned with the welfare of children, in the form of a set of criteria that are empirically correlated with measures of children's best interests. The primary criteria that stand out as the most important considerations, having a consistent effect across all measures, are those related to parenting. Despite the fact that these models show that children are resilient – the measure of every outcome is strongly predicted by the measure taken two years previously – it is also clear that parenting is crucial to children's success, even after controlling for the established traits in the child. Children's behaviour, in particular, is strongly affected by parenting, although smaller effects are noticed upon children's health and school performance as well. In terms of magnitude, the effects of physical punishment and 'yelling' at the child appear to have particularly strong, negative effects on children. This finding confirms results that researchers such as Straus (2001a, b) have been reporting for some time with respect to physical punishment of children, yet adds an important new finding on the relationship of yelling to children's well-being.

In order to provide a framework for those involved with custody assessment and children's welfare in general, I propose to group the factors in an ordinal fashion according to their relative impact on children's welfare. Of primary importance to children, according to the results achieved in this analysis, are behaviours involving *physical punishment* and *yelling or speaking in a raised voice* to children. The effect from these behaviours stands above all others in their impact on children, and should be of primary concern to assessors of children's interests. A secondary group of effects includes positive parenting practices such as *positive parental interaction* with children and the *consistent setting of boundaries* by parents. So, while the forms of punishment discussed above seem to have strong deleterious effects on children, it appears that consistent discipline remains very important for child well-being, as well as sharing positive times with children. Another factor of secondary importance is depression in a caregiver, which has a consistently negative effect on most measures of children's interests. While other aspects of mental health may well also be important predictors of children's outcomes, the data available did not allow testing of any condition but depression. Another factor of secondary importance is the structurally determined supervision or *parent-child ratio* in the family. While this factor does not affect all outcomes directly, it has very large direct effects on children's aggression and propensity to destroy property, both of which are of particular interest to criminologists. Moreover, supervision has important indirect effects on children's outcomes by reducing physical punishment and yelling, and by increasing positive interaction, although supervision also appears to decrease parental consistency. *Household income* is also a factor of secondary importance, even though both measures of income are of considerably less import than a direct linear effect of income would be. The most substantively important measure of income in these models is the base 10 logarithm of household income, which has both direct and indirect effects on children's outcomes. The log of household income has a very strong reducing effect on caregiver depression as well as on reducing the tendency to use physical punishment, although these effects require a tenfold increase in household income. So, while the factors of primary importance in children's well-being appear to be the reduction of physical punishment and yelling, positive parental interaction, consistency, caregiver depression, supervision, and household income are secondary factors that are important in creating beneficial outcomes for children.

Among variables which seem to have tertiary importance, *caregiver education* appears to have mild, mainly positive, direct effects on children's outcomes, along with positive indirect effects on children's outcomes, by increasing positive interaction and consistency while attenuating caregiver depression and physical punishment. An *intact, biological family*, even after controlling for other structural factors such as the parent-to-child ratio and custody changes, has important beneficial effects on hyperactivity and represents the most important effect on school performance. An intact family also has strong indirect effects on children's outcomes by reducing caregiver depression and increasing consistency, although there is also a smaller unfavourable effect through physical punishment and yelling. Not unexpectedly, a custody change does not appear to produce any direct benefits for children. While there appears to be some indirect benefits to a custody change to the father, this result should be treated with caution given the relatively small number of male caregivers in this sample. Even less impact appears to be attributable to *parental gender*, which appears to be the least important of all the variables measuring parental characteristics.

The foregoing represents an attempt to provide a ranking of factors that affect children in order to better arm those involved in custody determinations with a guide to the relative importance of different factors on children's outcomes. These models, however, serve to inform not only the factors by which children are affected, but also *how* these effects transpire. Three causal mechanisms were also tested to see which were useful in explaining how children's outcomes are created. Of these, there was evidence that both the direct model and the indirect or strain model were at play. That is, structural and household characteristics such as the parent-child ratio and household income can affect children directly and indirectly through strain on the parents. This finding lends some credence to the idea that policy makers and those interested in the welfare of children should take potential strains on parents into account when modifying the social contexts of families at risk.

While the above analysis has attempted to account for as many relevant variables as possible, there are some variables which, although important, were not accounted for. One of these, mental health measures other than depression, has already been commented on. But another variable relevant to the welfare of children that was not included in these models is inter-parental conflict. Previous studies have indicated that this variable explains at least part of the deficits in children associated with divorce. However, this variable is an attribute of a couple, not an individual parent, and so is of limited use in an analysis intended to be of use in evaluating custody. Nonetheless, future research could control for this theoretically relevant factor when modelling children's outcomes in the context of their families.

The findings of this study support some of the assumptions of custody evaluators and contradict others. For example, custody evaluators place an emphasis on parenting, which is strongly supported by the findings here – one of the important contributions this work has to make involves specifying which particular aspects of parenting are important for children and the relative benefits of each. Custody evaluators also stress issues such as parental alienation, the emotional bond with the child, and the psychological health of the parent. This research was able to confirm the importance of only one aspect of the parent's mental health – depression – but that finding confirms custody evaluators' beliefs that at least this aspect of parental mental health is important to children.

There was no measure in these models with respect to parental alienation; however, the paradigm proposed below would indicate that parental alienation is not in a child's interest. The measures in this model were behavioural, as opposed to emotional, and so no comment can be made on the importance placed by custody evaluators on the emotional bond between parent and child, although one measure – positive parental interaction with the child – could be correlated with the emotional bond, a potential subject for future research. Custody evaluators also place very little stock in the gender of the parent as an indicator of parental fitness, another tenet that is strongly supported by this research. On the other hand, custody evaluators place little emphasis on family structure, while the findings here suggest that this can be an important benefit for children: increases in the parent-child ratio are beneficial with respect to some aspects of children's behaviour and reduce the strain on parents, resulting in indirect benefits to children.

Many of the variables deemed important by Goldstein et al. (1996), such as the person who prepares meals or does laundry, were not measured in these models since they have no theoretical relevance to parental fitness. Moreover, there is no guidance from the originators of the primary psychological parent paradigm as to measures of the quality of these activities or their relative importance. Given the large number listed – a grab-bag of chores performed by housewives from the 1950s – it is difficult to use these criteria as a guide to evaluate custody, and to do so may contribute more to a gender stereotype than a true practical guide to parental fitness. Nevertheless, there can be little doubt that a certain minimum standard of care for a child is necessary for her or him to thrive. Failure to provide a minimum of care could be construed as neglect, although in the legal sense this must reach severe dimensions before it crosses the threshold of a court's attention. The degree to which a child receives the necessities of life under the care and management of a particular parent may be an important area for future research endeavours. Establishing guidelines as to the degree of care required along specific dimensions may well benefit children, whether or not they undergo a divorce of their parents, since minimum standards of care may establish a floor below which fewer children will fall. It may also help organizations aiming to help children at the low end of the socio-economic spectrum to develop programs designed to meet these children's needs.

Paradigms

The current dominant paradigm in the legal community with respect to custody determinations is known variously as the primary caregiver presumption, or the primary psychological parent, and prescribes selecting one parent who will be given complete discretion over all aspects of the child's upbringing. Thus, the current practice of custody determination is essentially a severance of the child from all supportive adult relationships but one. Any other relationships for the child are regarded as potential threats to the child's well-being and are allowed only upon the discretion of the custodial parent. This 'winner takes all' approach fosters inter-parental conflict by greatly increasing the stakes involved in divorce and severs the child from important supports that promote her or his development. The severance of a parental relationship upon divorce – a consequence of the primary caregiver paradigm – may be the most important source of deficits in children of divorce that is noted in many social science studies, perhaps even as much as the reliance on parental gender for custody that prevents the assignment of the best available parent (also promoted by primary caregiver).

An alternative, heretical paradigm espoused by groups composed mainly of fathers – referred to as shared parenting or equal parenting – advocates a legal presumption of the child spending equal time with each parent upon the dissolution of a marriage. While this paradigm has some improvements over the paradigm of primary caregiver, it is not applicable or practical in all situations and neglects issues related to extended family, such as grandparents. An alternative to these paradigms is one where parents, and all supportive adults including extended family members, be regarded as resources – social capital – available to children. The duty of the law under this paradigm is to ensure that children have the maximum benefit from these resources, taking into account the quality of parenting, parental characteristics such as mental health and education, and characteristics of family structure, formulating a post-divorce environment for a child that maximizes her or his access to the resources needed for development. Current research on this topic suggests that this framework corresponds with the best interests of children, based on studies of adult children of divorce, comparisons of joint versus sole legal custody, and recent data on participation of tasks within families (Kruk 2005). The connection of children to their parents needs to be treated as it is currently under child welfare laws: children are not removed from the care of their parents without cause. Moreover, establishing the child's biological heritage enables several important capabilities for the child in terms of legal rights, identity formation, and health management. This principle of connectedness would ensure that children of divorce are not deprived of a parent because of a divorce or because of the circumstances of their birth. Parents, in this regard, are constructed as a right of the child and would not be removed without cause. Through the maintenance of these relationships the engagement of extended family is also fostered.

Due to the difficulties of communication between parents post-divorce, it follows that communication channels to all relevant supportive adults from institutions concerned with children's welfare are of particular importance. Information that a child is having difficulty, be it of an educational, health, or behavioural nature, is more likely to open up resources to a child than the primary caregiver approach, which severs all such channels until opened by the custodial parent. Further, the protection of a child from abuse of all kinds is best prevented by providing as many sources of help for a child as possible and avoiding isolation of the child from his or her community of support. Custody assignment, under this paradigm, becomes a matter not of severing relationships, as it is at present, but of connecting children to the best resources in the optimal context possible under the circumstances. This paradigm is, I argue, one that can guide both legal principles and children's best interests, yet remain flexible enough to be adaptable to the specific needs of children and their families.

Other Explanatory Narratives

The highly imbalanced outcomes of custody with respect to gender is so prominent that many ad hoc narratives have been developed in order to explain the apparent reliance on gender with other variables not analysed here. While some of these narratives have underlying variables that call for investigation and further research, others are more fanciful. The first of these explanations follows a path akin to the following: since gender of the parent isn't related to parental fitness, then why should a strong correlation of custody outcomes to parental

Figure 6.1: Bias and distribution of ability

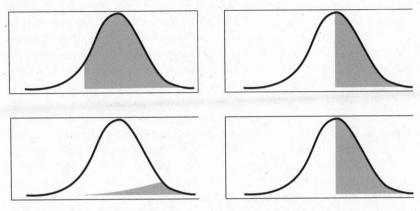

a) Ability (horizontal axis) distributed
equally with bias for selection.

b) Ability distributed evenly without
selection bias.

gender make a difference for children's welfare? A related narrative
involves the flipping of a coin: if either side of the coin is equally good,
why then should it matter which side it falls on? The rejoinder to these
stories is that although the gender of the parent is not a predictor of
parental ability, parental ability varies by individual, and so excluding
half of the available candidates means that children are not getting the
best available parent. If a coin always lands on one side, it isn't a fair
coin. Consider the situations represented in Figure 6.1. If there is no
gender bias and parenting ability is independent of gender, one would
expect the custody to be assigned as on the right (6.1b), where equal
numbers of mothers and fathers are awarded custody, the parents with
the higher than average parenting ability receiving custody. The
figures on the left (6.1a) illustrate the current situation, where mothers
gain custody most often, except where their parental ability is very
low. Selection of custody by an attribute uncorrelated with ability
results in less than optimal application of ability, despite the fact that
gender doesn't predict parenting ability. It *does* matter if the 'coin' is
fair.

Another narrative explaining the lopsided nature of custody outcomes could be characterized as a 'separate spheres' argument,
namely that outside of court, fathers freely relinquish custody of their
children, but if they dispute or contest custody, they are treated

equally at law. Most custody decisions are negotiated outside a court of law with varying degrees of legal involvement. The vast majority of custody orders are thus called 'consent' orders, which are merely ratified by a judge (as opposed to adjudicated). Hence, the explanation being offered here is theoretically possible. This represents an extremely unrealistic version of events, however, since divorce arrangements are negotiated within the constraints of the expected outcome in court. Moreover, the available evidence suggests that custody is at issue to some degree in the majority of divorces in Canada, whether negotiated outside of court or judicially determined (Department of Justice, Canada 1990). Moreover, the outcomes in court, while slightly improved compared to divorces without a hearing, are nonetheless highly unfavourable for fathers. For a more detailed treatment of this argument, see Millar and Goldenberg (1998). Nevertheless, there may be some degree of preference for maternal custody by both men and women as suggested by traditional gender roles, an aspect of agency within divorce that warrants further investigation.

Another explanation offered for mothers obtaining custody far more often than fathers is that judges do not want to disrupt the children, that they want to maintain a stable home environment for them. If mothers overwhelmingly establish interim custody compared to fathers, this would explain the highly skewed outcomes described in Chapter 2. The most difficult aspect of this explanation is that there is little research to support this contention, and hence it is an area worthy of further research. This explanation suffers from the same theoretical difficulties as the separate spheres argument. For example, mothers may be able to get an order for interim custody more easily than fathers, or fathers may realize that they are unlikely to obtain custody and so do not attempt to establish an equivalent home environment. In any event, the research here points to the best interests of the children being served by making the severance of custody from one parent or the other difficult to achieve.

Support

The analysis of the support data from the Survey of Labour and Income Dynamics (SLID) suggests that support payments, for many recipients and payors, represent only a small proportion of household income, with the mode of both the proportion paid and received being about

8.5 per cent. This figure hides the large amount of variability in the pro-portion of income dedicated to both payment and receipt of support. While it is difficult to make claims about the appropriateness of the amount received vis-à-vis the guidelines, since the paying and receiving households in this survey were not connected, the distribution of the proportion of income devoted to support payments suggests that the amounts are not well connected to the guideline amounts. Another finding of the analysis from Chapter 5 suggests that the income of those paying support varies significantly more than does the amount of support they pay. This is most likely due to the large resources in the forms of time, money, and emotional toll that are required to take a case to court. Because of these barriers, support awards appear to be drifting away from guideline amounts – since inflationary trends move salaries upwards on average, support awards would be expected to be, also on average, lower than the amount suggested by the guidelines. On the other hand, when income goes down, there is a strong likelihood that the payor will have difficulty having payments reduced to a level appropriate to his or her income. In this way, even if the guidelines are set to reasonable amounts, the system for their administration creates a regressive taxation situation, providing a relative reduction for those whose income increases while providing a relatively punishing increase for those who suffer income losses.

This state of affairs is largely due to the fact that the courts, as an institution, are ill equipped to manage the financial affairs of couples after divorce. Courts are designed to deal with matters of great importance that occur infrequently, thus justifying the enormous resources involved in court intervention. Since income varies, at least annually, and support is of secondary importance to both children and household income among those who receive it, the intervention of the court is justified neither by the impact nor by the staying power of the decision. Instead, the courts should consider developing an exit strategy for the management and assessment of child support amounts so that an institution, designed more like an agency of the executive branch such as Revenue Canada than of the courts, and more suited to the task, can be arranged.

Policy Implications

I will elaborate specifically here on policy implications, even though I have commented on such considerations in various places above. The first, and most obvious, policy implication for the judiciary of this work is that custody decisions must cease their reliance on gender as the primary determinative factor. While I have provided a ranked list of factors that are correlated with the best interests of children, a simple first step might be simply to provide the judiciary with feedback on the gender imbalances of their custody determinations on at least an annual basis; getting the judiciary to relinquish reliance on gender is the first step to getting them to rely on characteristics that benefit children. Although this research illustrates a continuing trend towards joint legal custody, legislators and superior courts might consider fostering a joint legal custody presumption. Joint legal custody is not related to a child's living arrangements, but rather, it is a device to enable communication related to a child's welfare to supportive adults. Moreover, awarding joint legal custody to other persons who are likely to be resources to children, such as extended family members where it is justified, could promote stronger support and potentially marshal assistance for a child at risk. Further, the benefits from the removal of legal impediments to communication will not be achieved unless education, health, and child welfare agencies are required to proactively release such information by legal or institutional policy. Thus, there must be a shift in paradigm from protecting the custodial parent's autonomy and privacy interests to connecting the child to a community of support. In terms of custody, there is one other policy implication and that is the use of split residential custody. While this recommendation is made somewhat more tentatively than the previous ones, it nonetheless appears to be worthwhile to consider cautiously the use of split custody in order to provide children with greater resources. This should not be undertaken in order to divide the children as if they were financial assets; rather, the empirical findings presented here suggest that one parent for each child might be more enabling than half a parent for two children together, other factors being equal.

Although the judiciary can make considerable improvement on its management of custody determinations, it is not institutionally suited to deal with the constantly changing area of child support: the courts should focus on issues that are of great import and that are relatively permanent once adjudicated. Child support just does not fit this description. The judiciary needs to develop a plan to extricate itself from support determination and allow it to pass into the domain of administrative law. In this situation, the courts will still be the ultimate arbiter of child support disputes through the appeal process, but will be removed from day-to-day governance issues. A similar opportunity might be available with respect to other family law issues. Family law mediation in particular promises to reduce parental conflict and be less of a financial strain on divorcing families and is in need of further research (Kelly 2004). An institution that deals with mediating divorce, with administrative appeal to the courts, would be less expensive and more effective for both families and society.

Finally, research here indicates that children would benefit if all parents – not just those undergoing divorce – had a better understanding of which parenting practices are most effective. In particular, the training of parents on how to discipline children without physical punishment or yelling is an area that could be addressed through public education in general, in conjunction with schools, and through classes provided to parents in anticipation of birth.

Taking It Further

While this research sheds some light on the factors related to children's best interests, there remains a great deal of research to be completed in this area. For example, although some studies suggest that certain psychological conditions in parents might have adverse affects on children, little has been done to test this theory, with clinical or population-based studies connecting mental health conditions with children's well-being. In addition to the area of mental health, measurements for parenting behaviour are particularly lacking. Not all relevant parental behaviours have measures, and some of the measures available are not ideal – for example, while the NLSCY measured physical punishment and yelling, it did so with only one question for each of these important concepts. The NSLCY includes a scale intended to measure rational parenting style, but even after examining all potential combinations of the items in this scale, no measure could be constructed that satisfied the tests for criterion validity. The concept of rational parenting style may well be a useful one; however, a good measure is required before it can be used in a model. Further, there may well be other theoretically pertinent concepts that have yet to be properly measured and their effects on children gauged. For example, the measures for yelling and corporal punishment were based on single questions when a scale for these measures would be preferable, since they are important empirically and conceptually.

Another important area that was not measured and thus eluded investigation was the role that access or visitation plays in the lives of children. Future data collection by Statistics Canada in this area promises to produce usable data for a key area of family law research. Moreover, further work could extend the relationship between demographic criteria and custody outcomes. This analysis shows an undue influence of gender in the determination of custody outcomes, much of which can be attributed to expected outcome in a court of law. However, there may be some degree of preference for maternal custody by both men and women as suggested by traditional gender roles, an aspect of agency within divorce that warrants further investigation. Whether or not this is the case, family law needs to develop a presumption that ensures children remain connected to their parents and to others who may be supportive in their development.

I set out in this work to investigate the effect of family law on Canadian children. In particular, it looks mainly at the effects of family law through the assignment of custody and finds that custody is assigned mainly on the basis of criteria that are unrelated to children's welfare, consequently falling short of its potential to provide the best possible outcomes for children, and, in this sense, acting against their interests. The work does not rest there, however – it aims to provide alternative criteria for selecting a custodial parent after divorce, criteria that do not rely on parental gender. Moreover, a new paradigm for thinking about children's best interests after divorce is presented that provides a context for future research. An investigation into child support suggests that the management of child support amounts post-divorce is an activity that the courts are ill-equipped to accomplish. This function would be better handled under administrative law by an agent of the executive branch, with less proximate involvement of the courts through administrative appeals.

It is my hope that, in the spirit of reform, the courts will undertake to renew their relevance and maintain the legacy of their important contribution to Canada's democratic tradition with respect to family law. The work presented here could be a starting point to that journey.

Notes

Introduction

1 See, for example, Gordon v. Goertz [1996] 2 S.C.R. 27; and Young v. Young [1993] 4 S.C.R. 3.
2 Of the categories explicitly assured of equality in section 15, only sex is separately protected in section 28.
3 Some data are available to the public, but these files do not connect children from one measurement (cycle) to another, and many data are excluded in order to protect the privacy of respondents.

2 Child Custody Outcomes in Canada

1 This variation of legal involvement is discussed in more detail below.
2 As a British colony, Canada's laws were by default British laws until separate legal norms and legislation were developed here.
3 Adultery is notoriously difficult to prove, so this proscription is not as restrictive as might be thought.
4 A detailed description of a nineteenth-century case is available: see Backhouse (1991).
5 I will deal more thoroughly with issues surrounding the birth of the child later on.
6 However, some courts have ruled that this is not a right of the non-custodial parent. A non-custodial parent made a human rights complaint because the Calgary Regional Health Authority refused access to his child's medical information. The court dismissed the complaint: see Sleiman v. Alberta Human Rights And Citizenship Commission and Calgary Regional Health Authority [2002], Alberta Court of Appeal No. 0201-0247AC.

7 Although divorces, like all court proceedings, are matters of public record and are therefore available to anyone upon request, there was a concern that providing identifying information might compromise the privacy of individuals.
8 Logistic regression.
9 Using multinomial logistic regression.
10 Statisticians refer to the most common outcome as the mode.
11 Prentice's unit of analysis was the case. The data shown here change the unit of analysis to the parent-children relation in order to be consistent with the current analysis.
12 Maximum likelihood regression.
13 These are defined above.

3 Explaining Children's Outcomes in the Context of Their Families

1 This database found citations or reviews in 819 volumes of law journals. Since volumes have many issues and some issues may have multiple references, the actual number of references is considerably greater than this.
2 The highest-ranking exceptions to this, according to a survey of judges (N=97), include allegations of sexual or physical abuse and parental fitness issues (Waller and Daniel 2004).
3 Pearson correlation values range from –1 (perfectly negatively correlated) to 0 (no correlation) to 1 (perfectly positively correlated); 0.9 indicates very strong positive correlation.

4 An Empirical Assessment of the Determinants of Children's Outcomes

1 Each collection or survey of data is called a cycle.
2 Also known as cross-sectional time series analysis.
3 A fuller description of the techniques used in this analysis may be reviewed elsewhere (Millar 2006).

5 The Effect of Child Support on Household Income
1 Family issues are subsumed under provincial jurisdiction in Canada; thus, the federal government can only coordinate provincial legislation. All provinces except Quebec, which has its own guidelines, have worked in conjunction with the federal government in the creation of these guidelines.
2 By 32 per cent on average (Finnie 1997).

3 Estimated at $410 million per year as of 1996. See Budget 1996: The New
   Child Support Package, Cat. No. F1-23/1996-6E (Ottawa: Department of
   Supply and Services Canada 1996), at 9.
4 Unless the children spend at least 40 per cent of the time with the non-
   custodial parent.
5 More than 95 per cent of support orders involve the payment of support
   by men to women (Statistics Canada 2005:26), an even greater gender
   imbalance than found in custody awards.
6 Compared to other factors such as parenting, parental depression, and
   parental supervision.
7 All figures are adjusted for weights such that the total number of cases
   represents the sample size, but the breakdown by any characteristic is
   representative of the population.
8 After adjusting for different taxation by province, the guidelines are
   the same in all provinces except Quebec, which has a different set of
   guidelines.

References

Statutes

An Act for the Relief of the Poor, 1601. Elizabeth 1, c. 2. 702.
An Act to Amend the Law Relating to the Custody of Infants (Talford's Act),
   1839, 2 & 3. Victoria. 179-80.
Charter of Rights and Freedoms, 1982. Canada Act 1982 (U.K.). c 11.
Custody of Infants Act, 1855. S.U.C.
Divorce Act, 1968. R.S.C., 1970.
Divorce Act, 1986. R.S.C., 1985.
Divorce Act, ss. 11 (1) (b) & 15(1)(3), 1986.
Divorce Act, s. 16 (4), 1986.
Domestic Relations Act. Revised Statutes of Alberta 2000.
Family Law Act, 2003. S5. 8–9. Revised Statutes of Alberta, 2003.

Cases

D.B.S. v. S.R.G.; L.J.W. v. T.A.R.; Henry v. Henry; Hiemstra v. Hiemstra [2006]
   2 S.C.R. 231.
Garska v. McCoy 278 S.E. 2d 357, 363 (W. Va. 1981).
Gordon v. Goertz [1996] 2 S.C.R. 27.
Keller v. MacDonald. 1998. "Keller v. MacDonald." *Unreported: Alberta Court
   of Queen's Bench Judgement No. 1294 AQB 9601-12622.*
Johnson-Steeves v. Lee. 1997. *Alta. L.R. (3d)* 54:218.
Levesque v. Levesque [1994] 20 *Alta. L.R. (3d)* 429.
Willick v. Willick [1994] 3 S.C.R. 670.
Young v. Young [1993] 4 S.C.R. 3.

Books and Articles

Abramowicz, Sarah. 1999. 'English Child Custody Law, 1660–1839: The Origins of Judicial Intervention in Paternal Custody.' *Columbia Law Journal* 99:1344–91.

Ackerman, Marc J. 2001. *Clinician's Guide to Child Custody Evaluations.* New York: John Wiley.

Ackerman, Marc J., and Mellissa C. Ackerman. 1997. 'Custody Evaluation Practices: A Survey of Experienced Professionals (Revisited).' *Professional Psychology: Research and Practice* 28:137–45.

Ackerman, Marc J., and K. Schoendorf. 1992. *The Ackerman-Schoendorf Parent Evaluation for Custody Test (ASPECT).* Los Angeles: Western Psychological Services.

Amato, Paul R. 1993. 'Children's Adjustment to Divorce: Theories, Hypotheses, and Empirical Support.' *Journal of Marriage and the Family* 55:23–38.

Amato, Paul R., and Joan G. Gilbreth. 1999. 'Nonresident Fathers and Children's Well-Being: A Meta-Analysis.' *Journal of Marriage and the Family* 61:557–73.

Amato, Paul R., and Juliana M. Sobolewski. 2001. 'The Effects of Divorce and Marital Discord on Adult Children's Psychological Well-Being.' *American Sociological Review* 66:900–21.

American Psychological Association. 1994. 'Guidelines for Child Custody Evaluations in Divorce Proceedings.' *American Psychologist* 49:677–80.

Aquilino, William S. 1994. 'Later Life Parental Divorce and Widowhood: Impact on Young Adults' Assessment of Parent-Child Relations.' *Journal of Marriage and the Family* 56:908–22.

Backhouse, Constance. 1991. Petticoats and Prejudice : Women and Law in Nineteenth Century Canada. Toronto: Osgoode Society/Women's Press.

Bailey, Martha J. 1995. 'England's First Custody of Infants Act.' *Queen's Law Journal* 20:391–437.

Bala, Nicholas, Kang Lee, Rod Lindsay, and Victoria Talwar. 2000. 'A Legal and Psychological Critique of the Present Approach to the Assessment of the Competence of Child Witnesses.' *Osgoode Hall Law Journal* 38:409–51.

Bala, Nicholas, K. Ramakrishnan, Rod Lindsay, and Kang Lee. 2005. 'Judicial Assessment of the Credibility of Child Witnesses.' *Alberta Law Review* 41.

Bauserman, Robert. 2002. 'Child Adjustment in Joint-Custody versus Sole-Custody Arrangements: A Meta-Analytic Review.' *Journal of Family Psychology* 16:91–102.

Beck, Ulrich, and Elisabeth Beck-Gernsheim. 2002. *Institutionalized Individualization: Individualism and Its Social and Political Consequences.* London: Sage.

Boyd, Neil. 1995. *Canadian Law: An Introduction*. Toronto: Harcourt Brace.

Brannigan, Augustine, and Christopher Levy. 1983. 'The Legal Framework of Plea Bargaining.' *Canadian Journal of Criminology* 25:399–419.

Braver, Sanford , and Diane O'Connell. 1998. *Divorced Dads: Shattering the Myths*. New York: Penguin Putnam.

Bricklin, Barry. 1995. The Custody Evaluation Handbook: Research-Based Solutions and Applications. Bristol, Pa.: Brunner/Mazel.

Brinig, Margaret F., and Douglas W. Allen. 2000. 'These Boots Are Made for Walking': Why Most Divorce Filers Are Women.' *American Law and Economics Review* 2:126–69.

Bushard, Phil. 1995. 'Interviewing Adults.' In *The AFCC Resource Guide for Custody Evaluators: A Handbook for Parenting Evaluations*, edited by Dorothy Howard and Phil Bushard. Madison, Wis.: Association of Family and Conciliation Courts.

Bushard, Phil, and Dorothy Howard (Eds.). 1995. *Interviewing Adults*. Madison, Wis.: Association of Family and Conciliation Courts.

Byrne, James G., Thomas G. O'Connor, Robert S. Marvin, and William F. Whelan. 2005. 'Practitioner Review: The Contribution of Attachment Theory to Child Custody Assessments.' *Journal of Child Psychology and Psychiatry* 46:115.

Cherlin, Andrew J., and Frank F. Furstenberg Jr. 1994. 'Stepfamilies in the United States: A Reconsideration.' *Annual Review of Sociology* 20:359–81.

Cherlin, Andrew J., Frank F. Furstenberg Jr., P. Lindsay Chase-Linsdale, Kathleen E. Kiernan, Philip K. Robins, Donna Ruane Morrison, and Julien O. Teitler. 1991. 'Longitudinal Studies of Effects of Divorce on Children in Great Britain and the United States.' *Science* 252:138689.

Coleman, James S. 1987. 'Families and Schools.' *Educational Researcher* 16:32–8.

– 1988. 'Social Capital in the Creation of Human Capital.' *American Journal of Sociology* 94:S95–120.

– 1990. *Foundations of Social Theory*. Cambridge, Mass.: The Belnap Press of Harvard University Press.

Daly, Martin, and Margo Wilson. 1988. *Homicide*. New York: Aldine De Gruyer.

Department of Justice, Canada. 1990. 'Evaluation of the Divorce Act: Phase II Monitoring and Evaluation.' Ottawa: Bureau of Review.

Donnelly, Denise, and David Finkelhorn. 1992. 'Does Equality in Custody Arrangement Improve the Parent-Child Relationship?' *Journal of Marriage and the Family* 54:837–45.

Ely, M., M.P.M. Richards, M.E.J. Wadsworth, and B.J. Elliott. 1999. 'Secular Changes in the Association of Parental Divorce and Children's Educational

Attainment: Evidence from Three British Cohorts.' *Journal of Social Policy* 28:437–55.

Evans, M.D.R., Jonathan Kelley, and Richard A. Wanner. 2001. 'Educational Attainment of the Children of Divorce: Australia, 1940–90.' *The Australian and New Zealand Journal of Sociology* 37:275–97.

Fabricius, William V. 2003. 'Listening to Children of Divorce: New Findings That Diverge from Wallerstein, Lewis, and Blakeslee.' *Family Relations* 52:385–96.

Fabricius, William V., and Sanford L. Braver. 2004. 'Expenditures on Children and Visitation Time: A Reply to Garfinkel, McLanahan and Wallerstein.' *Family Court Review* 42:350–62.

Fabricius, William V., Sanford L. Braver, and K. Deneau. 2003. 'Divorced Parents' Financial Support of Their Children's College Expenses.' *Family Court Review* 41:224–41.

Finnie, R. 1997. 'The Government's Child Support Package.' *Canadian Family Law Quarterly* 15:79–102.

Fox, Greer Litton, and Robert F. Kelly. 1995. 'Determinants of Child Custody Arrangements at Divorce.' *Journal of Marriage and the Family* 57:693–708.

Freiberg, Arie. 2006. 'Jurisprudential Miscegenation: Strict Liability and the Ambiguity of Law.' In *Critical Studies in Crime Control: Governance and Regulation in Social Life*, edited by Augustine Brannigan and George Pavlich. London: Glasshouse.

Friedman, Lawrence M., and Robert V. Percival. 1976. 'Who Sues for Divorce? From Fault through Fiction to Freedom.' *The Journal of Legal Studies* 5:61–82.

Furstenberg, Frank F. Jr. 1990. 'Divorce and the American Family.' *Annual Review of Sociology* 16:379–403.

Furstenberg, Frank F. Jr., Saul D. Hoffman, and Laura Shrestha. 1995. 'The Effect of Divorce on Intergenerational Transfers: New Evidence.' *Demography* 32:319–33.

Furstenberg, Frank F. Jr., and M.E. Hughes. 1995. 'Social Capital and Successful Development among At-Risk Youth.' *Journal of Marriage and the Family* 57:580.

Gardner, Richard A. 1998. *The Parental Alienation Syndrome.* Cresskill, NJ: Creative Therapeutics.

Goldstein, Jacob , and C. Abraham Fenster. 1994. 'Anglo-American Criteria for Resolving Child Custody Disputes from the Eighteenth Century to the Present: Reflections on the Role of Socio-Cultural Change.' *Journal of Family History* 19:35–56.

Goldstein, Joseph, Anna Freud, and Albert J. Solnit. 1973. *Beyond the Best Interests of the Child*. New York: The Free Press.
- 1979. Before the Best Interests of the Child. New York: The Free Press.
- 1986. *In the Best Interests of the Child*. New York: The Free Press.
Goldstein, Joseph, Albert J. Solnit, Sonja Goldstein, and Anna Freud. 1996. *The Best Interests of the Child*. New York: The Free Press.
Gordon, R., and L.A. Peek. 1988. *The Custody Quotient*. Dallas, Tex.: Willmington Institute.
Gorman-Smith, Deborah. 2003. 'Prevention of Antisocial Behaviour in Females.' In *Early Prevention of Adult Antisocial Behaviour*, edited by David P. Farrington and Jeremy W. Coid, 292–317. West Nyack, NY: Cambridge University Press.
Gottfredson, Michael R., and Travis Hirschi. 1990. *A General Theory of Crime*. Stanford, Calif.: Stanford University Press.
Gould, Jonathan W. 1998. Conducting Scientifically Crafted Child Custody Evaluations. Thousand Oaks, Calif.: Sage.
Gourley, E.V. III, and A.L. Stolberg. 2000. 'An Empirical Investigation of Psychologists' Custody Evaluation Practices.' *Journal of Divorce and Remarriage* 33:1–29.
Government of Alberta. 2005. 'Eligibility Criteria and Administration of the Resource Rebate.' Government of Alberta.
Gunnoe, Marjorie Lindner, and Sanford L. Braver. 2001. 'The Effects of Joint Legal Custody on Mothers, Fathers and Children Controlling for Factors that Predispose a Sole Maternal versus Joint Legal Award.' *Law and Human Behavior* 25:25–43.
Harris, Grant, Zoe Hilton, Marnie Rice, and Angela Wyatt Eke. 2005. 'Children Killed by Their Own Parents.' In *American Society of Criminology Annual Meeting*. Toronto.
Higgins, Chris, and Linda Duxbury. 2002. 'The 2001 National Work-Life Conflict Study: Report One.' Ottawa: Healthy Communities Division, Health Canada.
Hirczy, Wolfgang. 2000. 'From Bastardy to Equality: The Rights of Nonmarital Children and Their Fathers in Comparative Perspective.' *Journal of Comparative Family Studies* 31:231.
Hodges, William F. 1991. Interventions of Children of Divorce: Custody, Access and Psychotherapy. New York: Wiley.
Holland, Winifred. 2000. 'Intimate Relations in the New Millenium: The Assimilation of Marriage and Cohabitation?' *Canadian Journal of Family Law* 17:114–68.
Houghton, The Honorable Margaret M. 1995. 'The Court's View of Parenting

Evaluations.' In *The AFCC Resource Guide for Custody Evaluators: A Handbook for Parenting Evaluations*, edited by Dorothy Howard and Phil Bushard. Madison, Wis.: Association of Family and Conciliation Courts.

Hubin, Donald C. 1999. 'Parental Rights and Due Process.' *Journal of Law and Family Studies* 1:123–50.

Jacob, Herbert. 1992. 'The Elusive Shadow of the Law.' *Law and Society Review* 26.

Katkin, Daniel, Bruce Bullington, and Murray Levine. 1974. 'Above and Beyond the Best Interests of the Child: An Inquiry into the Relationship between Social Science and Social Action.' *Law and Society Review* 8:669–88.

Keilin, William G., and Larry J. Bloom. 1986. 'Child Custody Evaluation Practices: A Survey of Experienced Professionals.' *Professional Psychology: Research and Practice* 17:338–46.

Kelly, Joan B. 2004. 'Family Mediation Research: Is There Empirical Support for the Field?' *Conflict Resolution Quarterly* 22:37–53.

Kim, Eunjung. 2002. 'The Relationship between Parental Involvement and Children's Educational Achievement in the Korean Immigrant Family.' *Journal of Comparative Family Studies* 33:529–40.

Knafla, Louis. 1990. 'Law and Custom in Early Modern England.' In *La Coutoume = Custom*, edited by John Gilissen, 403–10. Bruxelles: De Boeck Université.

Kruk, Edward. 2005. 'Shared Parental Responsibility: A Harm Reduction-Based Approach to Divorce Law Reform.' *Journal of Divorce and Remarriage* 43:119–40.

Leikin, Sanford. 1995. 'First, Do No Harm.' *Ethics and Behaviour* 5:193.

Lisker, R., A. Carnevale, J.A. Villa, S. Armedares, and D.C. Wertz. 1998. 'Mexican Geneticists' Opinions on Disclosure Issues.' *Clinical Genetics* 54:321.

Maccoby, Eleanor E., and Robert H. Mnookin. 1992. *Dividing the Child: Social and Legal Dilemmas of Custody*. Cambridge, Mass.: Harvard University Press.

MacDonald, James C. 1986. 'Historical Perspective of Custody and Access Disputes: A Lawyer's View.' In *Custody Disputes: Evaluation and Intervention*, edited by Ruth S. Parry. Toronto: Lexington Books.

MacNaughton, H. Christina. 1995. 'The Attorney's View of Custody Evaluations.' In *The AFCC Resource Guide for Custody Evaluators: A Handbook for Parenting Evaluations*, edited by Dorothy Howard and Phil Bushard. Madison, Wis.: Association of Family and Conciliation Courts.

Marafiote, Richard A. 1985. The Custody of Children: A Behavioral Assessment Model. New York: Plenum Press.

Mauldon, Jane. 1990. 'The Effect of Marital Disruption on Children's Health.' *Demography* 27:431–46.

McBean, Jean. 1987. 'The Myth of Maternal Preference in Child Custody Cases.' In *Equality and Judicial Neutrality*, edited by Sheilagh Martin and Kathleen Mahoney. Toronto: Carswell.

McLeod, James Gary, and Alfred A. Mamo. 2001. 'Annual Review of Family Law.' *Annual Review of Family Law* 2001.

Millar, Paul. 2001. 'Non-Paternity in Canada.' *Department of Sociology*. Calgary: University of Calgary.

Millar, Paul, and Anne Gauthier. 2002. 'What Were They Thinking: The Development of the Canadian Child Support Guidelines.' *Canadian Journal of Law and Society* 17:139–62.

Millar, Paul, and Sheldon Goldenberg. 1998. 'Explaining Child Custody Determinations in Canada.' *Canadian Journal of Law and Society* 13:209–25.

– 2004. 'A Critical Reading of the Evidence on Custody Determinations in Canada.' *Canadian Family Law Quarterly* 21:425–35.

Miller, Jeffrey. 1997. *The Law of Contempt in Canada*. Scarborough, Ont.: Carswell.

Mnookin, Robert H. , and Lewis Kornhauser. 1979. 'Bargaining in the Shadow of the Law: The Case of Divorce.' *Yale Law Journal* 88:950–97.

Mortensen, Erik Lykke, Jente Andresen, Emil Kruuse, Stephanie A. Sanders, and June Machover Reinisch. 2003. 'IQ stability: The Relation between Child and Young Adult Intelligence Test Scores in Low-Birthweight Samples.' *Scandinavian Journal of Psychology* 44:395–98.

National Center for Health Statistics. 1996. *Vital Statistics of the United States, 1988*. Vol. III. *Marriage and Divorce*. Washington: Public Health Service.

Nims, Jerry P. 1995. 'Psychological Testing and Written Instruments.' In *The AFCC Resource Guide for Custody Evaluators: A Handbook for Parenting Evaluations*, edited by Dorothy Howard and Phil Bushard. Madison, Wis.: Association of Family and Conciliation Courts.

Novitski, Edward. 1977. *Human Genetics*. New York: Macmillan.

O'Donohue, W., and A.R. Bradley. 1999. 'Conceptual and Empirical Issues in Child Custody Evaluations.' *Clinical Psychology: Science and Practice* 6:310–22.

Olnyk, John K., Digby J. Cullen, Sina Aquila, Enrico Rossi, Lesa Summerville, and Laurie W. Powell. 1999. 'A Population-Based Study of the Clinical Expression of the Hemochromatosis Gene.' *The New England Journal of Medicine* 341:755–7.

Olweus, Dan. 1979. 'Stability of Aggressive Reaction Patterns in Males: A Review.' *Psychological Bulletin* 86:852–75.

Pearson, Jessica , and Nancy Thoennes. 1996. 'Acknowledging Paternity in
   Hospital Settings.' *Public Welfare* 5:44.
Perkins Gilman, Charlotte. 1998 [1898]. *Women and Economics: A Study of the
   Economic Relation between Men and Women as a Factor in Social Evolution.*
   Berkeley: University of California Press.
Peterson, R.R. 1996. 'A Re-Evaluation of the Economic Consequences of
   Divorce.' *American Sociological Review* 61.
Portes, Alejandro. 1998. 'Social Capital: Its Origins and Applications in
   Modern Sociology.' *Annual Review of Sociology* 24:1–24.
Prentice, B. 1979. 'Divorce, Children and Custody: A Quantitative Study of
   Three Legal Factors.' *Canadian Journal of Family Law* 2:358.
Quinnell, F.A., and J.N. Bow. 2001. 'Psychological Tests Used in Child
   Custody Evaluations.' *Behavioral Sciences and the Law* 19:491–501.
Sarat, Autin, and William L.F. Felstiner. 1995. *Divorce Lawyers and Their
   Clients.* New York: Oxford University Press.
Seltzer, Judith A. 1998. 'Father by Law: Effects of Joint Legal Custody
   on Nonresident Fathers' Involvement with Children.' *Demography*
   35:135–46.
Simons, Ronald L. 1996. Understanding Differences between Divorced and
   Intact Families: Stress Interaction and Child Outcome. Thousand Oaks,
   Calif.: Sage.
Skafte, Dianne. 1985. *Child Custody Evaluations : A Practical Guide.* Beverly
   Hills, Calif.: Sage.
Slate, John R., and Craig H. Jones. 1997. 'WISC-III IQ Scores and Special Edu-
   cation Diagnosis.' *Journal of Psychology* 131:119–20.
Snell, James G. 1991. *In the Shadow of the Law: Divorce in Canada 1900-1939.*
   Toronto: University of Toronto Press.
Spangler, Robert S., and David A. Sabatino. 1995. 'Temporal Stability of
   Gifted Children's Intelligence.' *Roeper Review* 17:203.
Spector, Paul E. 1992. *Summated Rating Scale Construction: An Introduction.*
   Newbury Park, Calif.: Sage.
Stack, Carol B. 1976. 'Who Owns the Child? Divorce and Child Custody
   Decisions in Middle-Class Families.' *Social Problems* 23:505–15.
Stahl, Philip Michael. 1999. *Complex Issues in Child Custody Evaluations.* Thou-
   sand Oaks, Calif.: Sage.
Statistics Canada. 2004. 'Divorces.' *The Daily* (4 May): 2–4.
Steinhauer, Paul D. 1993. *Guidelines for Assessing Parenting Capacity: Manual.*
   Toronto: Toronto Parenting Capacity Assessment Project.
Straus, Murray A. 2001a. *Beating the Devil Out of Them.* New Brunswick, NJ:
   Transaction.

– 2001b. 'New Evidence for the Benefits of Never Spanking.' *Society* 38:52–60.

Strayhorn, J.M., and C.S. Weldman. 1988. A Parent Practices Scale and Its Relation to Parent and Child Mental Health.' *Journal of the American Academy of Child and Adolescent Psychiatry* 27:613–18.

Talwar, Victoria, Kang Lee, Nicholas Bala, and Rod Lindsay. 2002. 'Children's Conceptual Knowledge of Lie- and Truth-telling and Its Relation to Their Actual Behaviors: Implications for Court Competence Examination.' *Law and Human Behavior* 26:395–416.

– 2004. 'Children's Lie-telling to Conceal Parents' Transgressions: Legal Implications.' *Law and Human Behavior* 28:411–35.

Thomson, Elizabeth, Thomas L. Hanson, and Sara S. McLanahan. 1994. 'Family Structure and Child Well-Being: Economic Resources vs. Parental Behaviors.' *Social Forces* 73:221–42.

Thorndike, R.L. 1933. 'The Effect of Interval between Test and Retest on the Constancy of the IQ.' *Journal of Educational Psychology* 24:543–49.

Turkat, Ira Daniel. 1999. 'Divorce-Related Malicious Parent Syndrome.' *Journal of Family Violence* 14:95–7.

Vasquez, Rosemary. 1995. 'Interviewing Children.' In *The AFCC Resource Guide for Custody Evaluators: A Handbook for Parenting Evaluations*, edited by Dorothy Howard and Phil Bushard. Madison, Wis.: Association of Family and Conciliation Courts.

Waller, Erika M., and A.E. Daniel. 2004. 'Purpose and Utility of Child Custody Evaluations: From the Perspective of Judges.' *Journal of Psychiatry and Law* 23:5–27.

Warshak, Richard A. 1992. The Custody Revolution: Father Custody and the Motherhood Mystique. New York: Simon and Schuster.

– 1993. 'How Children Fare in Father-Custody Homes.' *Family Advocate* 15:38–41.

Weitzman, Leonore. 1985. The Divorce Revolution: The Unexpected Social and Economic Consequences for Women and Children in America. New York: The Free Press.

Wertz, Dorothy C., John C. Fletcher, and John J. Mulvihill. 1990. 'Medical Geneticists Confront Ethical Dilemmas: Cross-cultural Comparisons among 18 Nations.' *American Journal of Human Genetics* 46:1200–13.

Whyte, William Foote. 1993[1943]. *Street Corner Society: The Social Structure of an Italian Slum*. Chicago: University of Chicago Press.

Zelizer, Virginia A. 1985. Pricing the Priceless Child: The Changing Social Value of Children. New York: Basic Books.

Index